CANON

AND

MISSION

Christian Mission and Modern Culture

EDITED BY
ALAN NEELY, H. WAYNE PIPKIN,
AND WILBERT R. SHENK

In the Series:

Trinity Press International, P.O. Box 1321, Harrisburg, PA 17105

Trinity Press International is a division of The Morehouse Group.

Cover design: Brian Preuss

Library of Congress Cataloging-in-Publication Data

Beeby, H. D.
    Canon and mission / H.D. Beeby.
        p. cm. — (Christian mission and modern culture)
    Includes bibliographical references.
    ISBN 1-56338-258-X   (pbk. : alk. paper)
    1. Missions—Biblical teaching.   2. Bible—Canonical criticism.   3. Missions—Theory.   I. Title.   II. Series.
    BV2073.B44   1998
    266'.001—dc21   98–48845
                                                          CIP

Printed in the United States of America
99   00   01   02   03   04   6   5   4   3   2   1

CANON
AND
MISSION

H. D. BEEBY

TRINITY PRESS
INTERNATIONAL
HARRISBURG, PENNSYLVANIA

Contents

6.78

Preface to the Series

Both Christian mission and modern culture, widely regarded as antagonists, are in crisis. The emergence of the modern mission movement in the early nineteenth century cannot be understood apart from the rise of technocratic society. Now, at the end of the twentieth century, both modern culture and Christian mission face an uncertain future.

One of the developments integral to modernity was the way the role of religion in culture was redefined. Whereas religion had played an authoritative role in the culture of Christendom, modern culture was highly critical of religion and increasingly secular in its assumptions. A sustained effort was made to banish religion to the backwaters of modern culture.

The decade of the 1980s witnessed further momentous developments on the geopolitical front with the collapse of communism. In the aftermath of the breakup of the system of power blocs that dominated international relations for a generation, it is clear that religion has survived even if its institutionalization has undergone deep change and its future forms are unclear. Secularism continues to oppose religion, while technology has emerged as a major source of power and authority in modern culture. Both confront Christian faith with fundamental questions.

The purpose of this series is to probe these developments from a variety of angles with a view to helping the church understand its missional responsibility to a culture in crisis. One important resource is the church's experience of two centuries of cross-cultural mission that has reshaped the church into a global Christian *ecumene*. The focus of our inquiry will be the church in modern culture. The series (1) examines modern/postmodern culture from a missional point of view; (2) develops the theological agenda that the church in modern culture must address in order to recover its own integrity; and (3) tests fresh conceptualizations of the nature and mission of the church as it engages modern culture. In other words, these volumes are intended to be a forum where conventional assumptions can be challenged and alternative formulations explored.

This series is a project authorized by the Institute of Mennonite Studies, research agency of the Associated Mennonite Biblical Seminary, and supported by a generous grant from the Pew Charitable Trusts.

Editorial Committee

ALAN NEELY
H. WAYNE PIPKIN
WILBERT R. SHENK

1

The Recovery of Scripture

Introduction

The story is told of Robert Benchley's first visit to Venice. Within a few minutes of arrival he had cabled his secretary: "All roads flooded, please advise." Recently, my wife and I went to Venice for the first time. A few people gave us advice before we went. The advice was always the same: "Don't buy a cup of coffee in St. Mark's Square because it will cost you five pounds if you do." So we didn't buy coffee in St. Mark's Square. Instead we went into St. Mark's. It was free.

The experience of going into St. Mark's remains fresh in my mind. You go into this twelfth-century, Byzantine building, and you are surrounded by golden mosaic. You first enter the immense portico, and there above you is creation. Then you walk down the nave, and you are surrounded by scripture in gold mosaic on the walls and on the ceiling. As you walk on, you move toward the altar—the cross, the place where the bread and wine of the sacrament are distributed. You are being oriented. You are surrounded by scripture. You are in the world of scripture, and you are facing the One to whom scripture points—the focus and the explanation of scripture. This is your orientation. You are being oriented because you are facing east, but much more profoundly you are being oriented because you are in the scriptural world and are facing that ultimate reality to which the scriptures point.

When you turn to leave that obvious biblical world, the cross is behind you, and on the west wall you see the last judgment. Now you are faced with the possibility of disorientation.

St. Mark's made a tremendous impression upon me. You may think that I am a nostalgic medievalist. I am not. I am not longing for a return to antiquity. The experience in St. Mark's sets the stage for what I want to address in this book.

St. Mark's speaks of the blessings of Christendom. Nowadays in Europe we are fully aware that Christendom has ended. Intellectually we know it and perhaps have no regrets. But Christendom stood for something. It stood for a whole continent that was dominated by the worldview of the Bible, and for about a thousand years Europe was held together by that worldview.

This is not to say that the Venetians were not sinners. They were sinners. Less than a mile from St. Mark's is the Rialto, where the merchant of Venice, Antonio, was possibly spitting on Shylock's beard. Venetians were sinners, but in that world they knew that when they sinned they could be forgiven in the church. Outside the church the same worldview held sway. The worldview of the Bible, which was not confined to the "believers," dominated the public life as well as the private. So I want first to hold up Christendom as pointing in some sense to an ideal of living totally within the worldview of the Bible.

Second, I want to use St. Mark's to emphasize that I am a European. The European situation has altered profoundly since the twelfth century, but much of that unraveling of Christendom has taken place in my lifetime, and the paganization of Europe is quickening. It has altered very much in the last ten years. I want to stress that I live now in a post-Christendom, postmodern Europe—a Europe that is becoming more and more pagan. However, that secular paganism is mixed with a growing religiosity, a religiosity that is a threat rather than an ally of Christian faith. That is the second thing St. Mark's says to us.

Third, St. Mark's speaks to us of the curse of Christendom. When you went out of St. Mark's you went into the world, but it was the world that was dominated by the biblical view. It was all Christendom, and therefore there was no need for a mission. To me, now, Christendom represents not only a blessing and an ideal; Christendom represents a curse. It is a curse on Europe, and it may be a curse on you, because in Europe the ghost of Christendom is still there although the reality is gone. And the ghost tends to suggest to people that we live in a culture that is companionable, that we live in a culture that is supportive of Christianity. This is a falsity, for the culture is more enemy than friend.

Christendom left us with a church that does not realize that the church exists for mission. It presented us with a God who is not the God of the *missio dei*. It obscured and concealed the fact that God is a missionary God and that the church exists for mission. It obscured the fact that theology is the handmaid of mission. And it obscured the fact that the Bible from Genesis to Revelation, if taken as a unity, is a handbook of mission. Unfortunately, we have a theology in Europe that is almost completely innocent of mission.

Fourth, I want to stress that the experience in St. Mark's pointed to the kind of methodology that I am using. I spoke of walking in a scriptural milieu, of being oriented there and then being disoriented. What I am doing here is not "missiology," not "biblical studies," not "theology." I am speaking as a missionary, walking, living, trying to ask missionary questions, practical missionary questions, and to bring them to the Bible. If there is any missiology, if there is any theology, if there is any biblical study, that is secondary.

I am trying to walk in the atmosphere of the Bible and to ask questions.

The purpose of this book is to state a proposal with sufficient clarity that hearers will be able to comment on it and to criticize it. I propose to bring together the canon of scripture in its entirety and the whole mission committed to the church. Such an ambitious undertaking needs explanation and some attempt at justification if I am not to be accused of either an excess of zeal or a lack of wisdom.

The need to voice such a proposal has been gestating slowly over a period of several years and has developed not so much out of academic curiosity as out of practical necessity and a sense of compulsion that had its clearest beginnings in 1971. In that year, an attempt to be faithful to Christ's mission, as I understood it, propelled me and some Taiwanese colleagues toward activity that was largely motivated by current interpretations of the Exodus. I was one of many throughout the world and throughout the ages who heard in the Exodus a promise of liberation and freedom. The promise became a command that had to be obeyed. Its authority was absolute and brooked neither compromise nor disobedience.

At the same time, I was constantly aware that this particular interpretation of the Exodus was both partial and flawed. I was even more aware that there were passages in the Bible that spoke very differently, passages that enjoined patience and resignation rather than political involvement.

Over against the Exodus theology, there was an equally insistent Exile theology expressed most clearly in Jeremiah's letter to the exiles in chapter 29. While moving obediently and irrevocably in one direction, I was daily conscious that I could be equally obedient to parts of scripture if I were moving irrevocably in the opposite direction. It was as though morning by morning God wakened one ear saying "Follow Moses," while the other ear was roused with "Why not Jeremiah 29?" The problem of canon and mission was already with me in its fullness. Autobiography has slowly blossomed into "theology."

My experience of religious certainty combined with conceptual contradiction has developed far beyond the remembrance of things past and now demands at the very least serious consideration and careful examination. If it is wrong to hope for solutions to the major problems, perhaps I might attempt to make more explicit the nature and form of some of the problems. My personal and local struggle with the use of canon and mission now points me to issues that seem to be very close to the heart of the Christian gospel and, therefore, important to Christian theology and integral to the church's life.

Both canon and mission, in recent times rarely explicitly linked together, now appear to me to be inseparable, distinguished in thought but not in practice. As in a love affair, they attract each other. The one attracts the other, and each is propelled toward, the other. Decades of teaching the Old Testament have convinced me of the need to interpret it in the light of the New Testament and vice versa, that is, to interpret canonically. The very expression Old Testament implies New Testament. The New Testament is theologically prior to the Old Testament, and the latter, as distinct from the "Hebrew Scriptures," is in part a creation of the New Testament. Each book or fragment of a book in the Bible can be read in many contexts. I am now certain that the most significant context is the theological context of the entire Bible read in the present and read missiologically. This must take precedence over any of the possible historical, literary, or other contexts that present themselves.

In trying to discover what it means to interpret canonically, I have learned a little of the mysterious nature of biblical unity. In particular, I have learned that the more one enters the mystery of that unity the more one is pointed in the direction of mission. A Bible atomized and fragmented can provide little sense of direction. But once the pieces are seen to be parts of a mighty whole, one realizes that this great totality has a clear focus and that it coincides with what we know as mission.

If the canon is gradually revealed as propelling its readers toward mission, can the reverse be said to be true? Does the church's mission in any way clamor for canonical understanding? Quite obviously it does. Many reasons could be given, but at this stage one will suffice. The missions of the various churches or segments of churches are often quite different in their emphases and ethos. Indeed, "different" is an understatement. In some cases they are polarized, and frequently the polarization is caused by or at least aided by reliance on certain biblical texts viewed in distorting isolation. Missions choose and adhere to particular models in their mission work according to whether, for example, they turn most readily to Matthew 28 or Matthew 25 or Luke 4 or the Exodus or several other texts or clusters of texts. Church planters rarely quote the Exodus, and liberation theologians are not enchanted by images of brands being plucked from the burning or escapees from the flood clambering onto the ark. Each part of the church or each missionary movement tends to build upon a selected text and its close relatives or, more disastrous still, builds upon fashion, prejudice, or ideology and then decorates the resulting structure with texts subjectively and arbitrarily chosen.

Is there then any way of avoiding the hazards of such prejudicial selectivity that can, on occasion, hinder the mission of Christ rather than advance it? Or if these dangers are inherent in the missionary task, are there means of making the church more aware of their presence and therefore forewarned and forearmed against them?

The answer, I submit, is in the canon. But to extract the answer is by no means easy, for it involves some form of canonical interpretation. Is it possible to move a little way toward a canonical interpretation that is at least aware of some of the hazards and endeavors to build bulwarks against them? A noncanonical interpretation is almost by definition heretical, because it means you have chosen a part of a greater whole without struggling to discover how the part relates to the whole. Is it representative of the whole, or is it a minority opinion? Is it a fragment or part of a continuing theme? Or is it a voice from the opposition benches in the biblical parliament? Is it prophetic or priestly, charismatic or kingly? Is it creation or redemption, saving history or wisdom, heterodox or orthodox? Is it part of one of the ongoing biblical dialogues, and if it is, what is its place in the dialogue? The questions it would be necessary to ask are numerous, and to ask them is only a fraction of what is involved in canonical interpretation.

I hope the concerns I have raised are sufficient to indicate that there is a case to be made for saying that contemporary mission, whether at home or abroad, can be seen as pointing out the need and significance of a canonical understanding of scripture. So far I have given two areas of motivation for the proposed study. The canon calls for mission, and mission has need of the canon.

To these I would add a third, although strictly speaking it is not an independent motive but a subdivision of the second because it arises within the demands of mission. Nevertheless, its importance requires that it receive separate mention. Since the demise of Christendom, it is increasingly recognized that there exists what might be termed "mission to culture." By this I mean culture at its deepest level. I'm not speaking of culture that prefers Beethoven over jazz. Nor am I talking about culture in the sense of Scottish culture—kilts and haggis—or Welsh culture—the leek and the daffodil. I am talking about culture on the deepest possible level: presuppositions, hidden preunderstandings, what we take for granted, what we see through rather than what we see.

I am talking about a particular mission to Western culture, not Western culture only as it is found in the West, but modern Western culture as it is increasingly found dominating the public life of almost every nation. To be truly Christian—that is, mission that proclaims the lordship of Christ in the public sphere as well as in the private sphere—this culture mission would have to be rooted in the New Testament. At the same time, because culture mission is concerned with national and international relationships, with political, social, commercial, military, educational, economic, and fiscal affairs—indeed, with the whole presuppositional infrastructure and the more visible superstructure of the nations—it would have to draw greatly upon the resources of the Old Testament, which is so richly endowed in these matters. This will require a canonical hermeneutic that is not content only with theory. It must be a hermeneutic that penetrates the secular as well as the religious realm. And it will provide direction and norm not only for conceptualization but also for ethical decision making for both the public and private spheres that is normative, missiological, and canonical.

In writing the above, I am conscious of numerous voices speaking to me from various periods of the church's history, and all of them are saying explicitly or implicitly, "We've been here before. Deja vu!" They point out that the canon is there precisely to be understood canonically and that we should have no mission at all if it had not been interpreted missiologically. Of course, we should avoid having a canon within the canon. Ever since Moses ascended Sinai and received the Commandments, it has been known that the word of the Lord was determinative for faith and works in the whole of life, whether private or public. Why then, the voices ask, is it thought necessary to restate what everyone knows? Apart from the possibility that perhaps not everyone does know, three reasons can be given for examination and restatement.

The first is obvious: although we may know, we may not remember, or if we remember we may not obey. The second is that some within the church would not so readily agree that this is what the church has always said at all times and in all places. And, if this were the case, they would say that that is where the church has been deeply wrong. The third reason, the patent one, is that even the eternal verities need to be restated in new ways for new days because the old statements sound strange, even unwelcome, in new contexts. Moreover, some new contexts may be total strangers to both eternity and verity. It is this third reason that demands and deserves most attention.

The Death of Scripture

All that follows depends upon what is meant by the canon. A fuller treatment than is possible here would have copious references to the array of current literature about canon. Few such references will appear, because in the limited space available I intend to approach canonical questions from a rather novel viewpoint, namely, that of missiology. This is being done with the hope that the missiological approach to canon may supplement the different and far greater canonical endeavors of others. Second, those aware of the literature will themselves easily recognize both my indebtedness to other writers and my inadequate reading of them.

The word *canon* usually points the mind in two distinct directions. First, it signifies the extent of a literature; it points to the fact that it is limited and defined, exclusive and inclusive, and that there is a general understanding and agreement as to where the bounds of the literature should be set. The second direction is that of power, influence, and authority; that is, by what right and with what force does the canon in question say what it does?

The question of the biblical canon's extent is of course problematic and controversial. There are several canons. Furthermore, all biblical quantification—for example, the number of Israel's tribes, the number of Christ's apostles—

is always a little uncertain. It wasn't recent mathematicians who invented fuzzy sets. The Bible invented fuzzy sets a long time ago. If the biblical writers had made chocolates, they would have had hard centers and soft outsides.

The second direction, that of authority, is the greater issue because it is inseparable from the issue of the nature of revelation in the Bible. What, precisely, is the Bible? Although accepting that I cannot assume any kind of consensus about the answer to such a question, I do assume that today in the West there is agreement that the nature of the Bible is problematic in the extreme. Where previously the Bible posed problems and raised problems, it has for some time been itself a problem. At one time it occupied a place in the West, where it was the supreme source of authority, criticism, and judgment. Now it is better known as just one of the many things from the past that are questioned, criticized, and judged according to standards and norms extant in the contemporary culture. These standards and norms are axiomatically taken to be more authoritative and therefore more qualified to question the Bible than the Bible is to question them. The Bible, once authoritative because divine in origin, now possesses dubious authority. And this holds not only outside the church but in many parts of the church as well.

The canon as the norm for mission inevitably functions according to the nature of the status of the norm. What then is the present situation regarding this norm? If the extent of the canon can be determined by tradition, its authority and present status certainly cannot. Before discussing its missionary implications, further consideration of its standing is necessary. This I propose to do by using partial synonyms, "Bible" and "scripture." If the canon is to function authoritatively, it can do so by assuming not only agreement about its extent but also by discovering, discerning, and describing the "Bible" and "scripture" and finding out how they are faring in the present.

In post-Enlightenment, post-Christendom, postmodernity, language is increasingly unreliable, especially religious
language. Words like "religion," "belief," "mission," "spiritual," "theology," "God" have become increasingly indeter-
minate. This invites caution when we consider "Bible" and
"scripture." However, because many other words are
dependent for their meaning on the values given to them by
"Bible" and "scripture," and because "canon," "scripture,"
and "Bible" are inseparable, we must attempt to clarify the
meaning we intend to give to "Bible" and "scripture." Some
European biblical scholars are either discussing the death of
scripture (Morgan and Barton 1988:chap. 2) or saying, as
scholars, that scripture is not their business. Their business
is to study the Bible, assuming that the Bible is one scripture among many others and that all are equally human creations (Smith 1993). But is scripture indeed dead, and what
do we mean by "scripture"? Why entitle this chapter "The
Recovery of Scripture"?

Scripture: Meaning and Recovery

If indeed scripture is, in some sense, lost, what might be
involved in its recovery? Certainly it would demand
immense scholarship, great endeavor, faith, and commitment, not to mention a time span measured in decades. It
would also demand a new concept of mission. Below I suggest a little of what that mission would require.

   Why does scripture need to be recovered? Who lost it?
In postmodern culture, where all the root paradigms are
antipathetic to scriptural claims, how does one say "scripture" and mean it? I believe there are only two sets of conditions under which "scripture" can be said seriously.

   The first was in the thousand-year period ending in the
seventeenth or eighteenth centuries in Europe, when the
general worldview and cultural infrastructure coincided
with those of scripture because they were formed by scripture. During this long period, the conflict between unity

and diversity in scripture was not unknown; the tensions, wherever you looked in the Bible, were very apparent. Scholars were not fools. But tension was maintained and accepted, and the unity was assumed in such a way that the multiplicity was held together so that parts were parts of a whole and not disparate fragments.

It was this unity that provided the worldview that gave consensus to society and around which Christendom was fashioned. It was this unity within the unity of the Trinity and the unity of the church that gave us the first universities— some of the same universities that now implicitly, if not explicitly, deny the faith that gave them birth. These universities now live by other novel faiths that turn them into pluriversities. Within such a complete and acknowledged unity the Bible was "scripture"; but scripture was rarely defined, because it was the source of definition, and its unity was rarely questioned because there was little to question it by. In such a world, "scripture" could be said and sincerely meant and easily understood.

The second set of circumstances are those that belong to post-Christendom and now are virtually ubiquitous. They are our circumstances, at least in Europe. They are in some ways circumstances similar to those of the early church; that is, where the church and the Bible exist in alien and unsympathetic territory, where the faith and some assumptions necessary to salvation are excluded and opposed in varying degrees and in varying ways. Despite the very obvious disadvantages, this can be seen as at least a partial advantage, because the very opposition helps to clarify what Christendom has concealed—namely, that the church is a colony; that the inevitable dissent from and eccentricity to the culture are of its nature and essence; and Christians are strangers and resident aliens. Christendom also concealed the fact that the church exists for mission and the scriptures are the account of the *missio dei*; that is, they arise out of mission and are intended for mission because they are the word of the missionary God. In today's scripture-excluding world, the church too long has been saying "scripture" but not really meaning it, except in an attenuated way. We have said "my scripture," "the church's scripture," "true for me," "true for the believer," "true for the church," "true for the heart but not for the head." In countless ways we have deceived ourselves, pretending we are still in Christendom and that the culture is our companion. Or, conceding postmodernity, we have accepted that every story is a little story among other little stories, each containing some truth among other little truths, because there is no true Truth. Or perhaps we just avoid the truth question altogether and settle for pragmatism or experience. Scripture has been virtually lost because it cannot truly be said within the presuppositions of contemporary culture that deny its proper worth.

"Bible" and "Scripture"

Sometimes we use the words "Bible" and "scripture" interchangeably, but not always. In a university or college or bookshop, it is more common to use "Bible" because the meaning is clear. It is a volume containing (for Protestants) sixty-six books. It is printed and sold like any other volume. Historians, booksellers, and even sociologists can say "Bible" without confusion or embarrassment. "Scripture" is different. First, it is a word that is rarely defined. Other religions use it and give it other meanings, but when Christians use it the meaning is hard to pin down.

Just like the word "Bible," the word "scripture" on occasion can also merely refer to the same volume of sixty-six books; but that is not all it does. Unlike "Bible," it is not much used in universities and bookshops, at least in Europe. It is "churchy," and is used, I suspect, much more often by evangelicals than liberals. Not just descriptive, it has an aura of faith about it and usually implies a value judgment that limits its usage to those who are prepared to affirm that it is authoritative and that this authority is a divine authority. It comes close to affirming that these sixty-six human books are a book containing the word of God.

What Is "Scripture"?

I have tried to define scripture. It is not easy to find definitions of scripture because we have felt defining it unnecessary. Let me try out my definition of scripture, because what I say afterward rather depends on its being not too far from the truth. The following six points attempt to express what is understood to be an orthodox and traditional view.

1. The word "scripture" can be said only after we have said "I believe" to the historic Christian faith, because the Bible only becomes scripture when it is seen as inseparable from the Trinity and the church.

2. Scripture has arisen within the church and can be truly understood only within the faith of the church. If it is read outside the faith of the church, there is a veil over the face of the reader.

3. Scripture is understood to be authoritative because ultimately it is not the creation of the church but of God. It is in human language written by humans, but it is also the word of God.

4. Scripture is a unity and must be read as a unity. Its authority belongs to the whole, and every part has authority only as part of the whole. If there is no united whole from Genesis to Revelation, then there can be no parts, because parts are parts only if each part is part of the whole. Without a whole there are only fragments, and fragments have no authority, just as a bone has no life or a severed hand no strength.

5. Scripture must be read as a Christ-centered, Christ-witnessing, unified narrative conforming to a trinitarian rule of faith.

6. Scripture is true for the whole world because Christ is Lord of all and not only Lord of the church. Only within the faith of the church can this limitless truth be recognized; nevertheless, the church must proclaim it as universal. To say "it is true for me" or "it is true for the church" is both contradictory and a denial of scriptural truth; that is, if these expressions imply a limited truth.

Whatever Happened to Scripture?

I believe that part of our present confusion, and the source of many of our problems, is that at one time all of Europe (good churchgoers and the rest) had a "scripture" and a "Bible" and that the two words and ideas were quite reasonably interchangeable. In saying this I am not idealizing the past or whitewashing the church or the Middle Ages. I am merely stating a fact about European culture, life, and literature in general up to the seventeenth and eighteenth centuries. Europe, quite simply, possessed a total worldview that was predominantly the worldview of the Bible. The Bible was held to be scripture, authoritative not only for individuals and for the church but for everybody and for the whole of society. The Bible, with its creator and redeemer, its heaven and hell, its judgment and afterlife, its Ten Commandments and moral precepts, provided the thought world and symbolic universe in which all living and dying took place. Scripture supplied the final pattern, norm, and goal for everything, and theology was the queen of the sciences.

Especially theology was the queen of the sciences. Christian theology ruled in the universities and the schools, which were extensions of the church. Chaucer and his pilgrims lived in the world of the Bible. So did Milton and Shakespeare, and Shakespeare was not a notorious churchgoer. So did Isaac Newton. They couldn't escape it. It was the mental air they breathed. It provided explanation; it determined what was true and false, right and wrong, good and bad; it ruled scholarship.

In such a world, the Bible unquestionably was scripture, and it was studied within the faith of the church because there was no real alternative. The Bible and the faith of the church were not only determinative for morality, economics, and politics; they determined scholarly excellence and all other excellences.

All this began to change in the seventeenth and eighteenth centuries. For many reasons, God and the Bible were removed from public life, from economics, politics, commerce, and science. In place of God and God's revelation, scholarship substituted objectivity, reason, secular thought, scientific truth, historical criticism, and much else. The scriptural worldview became a ghetto-option for those who in whole or in part chose to be aliens and eccentrics within the new culture and somehow fearfully and insecurely, confusedly and ambiguously, held on to some idea of scripture with as much of their minds as was possible.

If we Christians in post-Christendom really are confused and fearful aliens and eccentrics and have become so because of cultural change, can more be said about the nature of the change? And are we all—liberal, evangelical, Roman Catholic—in the same boat? I believe we are in different boats (the liberal Protestant one leaks the most), but we are all in boats in the same storm. I offer a few oversimplistic impressions of recent life in the two boats that most of us know best.

In the Liberal Boat

I speak first of from the liberal boat because I've been a crew member of it until not too long ago. In a sense, I can speak with a certain authority about the liberal boat. (When I come to the conservative boat, I speak as a sympathetic outsider.) In the liberal boat, the following has been overheard often during the last one hundred fifty years:

1. "We must not stand on the Bible and question the culture; we must stand within the culture and question the Bible."

2. "Our new enlightened understanding of unity will not permit us to regard the Bible as a unity."

3. "The Bible deserves the best scholarship. Therefore it must be moved from the house of faith to the house of reason." This position split the liberal mind because in the church it was hearing, "If you do not believe you cannot understand." But in the classroom it was hearing, "If you believe you cannot understand."

4. "The Bible was written by humans; therefore it is only human and must be studied as such."

5. "We must analyze and dissect." Result: dismemberment and demise.

6. "The historical context of the sections is all important. The contexts are very varied, thus making the sections independent of each other." Result: fragmentation and loss of authority.

7. "We now know that history did not happen as the Bible says. How then can it be scripture?"

8. "Preachers must study with reason but preach with faith." Result: gospel-loss, social gospel, resignation and resignations, burnout.

In the Conservative Boat

The following are the thoughts of a sympathetic outsider:

1. Conservatives tried to stand firm on the Bible, but they did not adequately question the culture. The resistance was faithful but not sufficiently thoughtful.

2. Confronted by the cultural onslaught, they increasingly tended to retreat from an evil world, made a virtue of personal piety, and left the world to the flesh and the devil.

3. Personal piety combined too easily with the new cultural individualism.

4. Faced with new tensions, they neglected God's creation and concentrated on redemption, just as liberals,

unsure of a revealed redemption, concentrated on the created world that they could see.

5. Fazed by new epistemologies, new understandings of history, and rampant positivism, they retreated (as did liberals, but in different ways) into personal experience. Growing "intellectual atheism" encouraged abandonment of the mind in favor of the heart.

6. Many of the above influences tended to produce canons within the canon. The social and political implications of the Old Testament were neglected and, de facto if not de jure, there were strong Marcionite tendencies and other forms of atomism and fragmentation.

7. Using the same new understanding of history as that of the liberals, they said, "The Bible is the word of God, therefore everything happened precisely as it states." But that was a post-Enlightenment statement. If they had been real traditionalists, they might have used allegory and more imagination.

What I've been saying about the two boats are mere hints, but even in their brevity they point to something singular and unexpected, at least unexpected to me. It is that differing, even opposite wings of the church, under the hammer of the new culture, in varying ways all produced—to coin a phrase—de-scripturizing elements: fragmentation, canons within the canon, a privatized church, blindness to idolatry within the culture, neglect of the Old Testament, a weakened ecclesiology, a loss of biblical unity, a limiting historicism, the excessive significance of personal experience, and a failure to realize that we speak of a scripture we no longer possess. Almost all of Protestantism opted for a personal belief within a privatized church. The gospel ceased to be public truth, and the word "scripture" became a kind of lip service to a lost past.

If there is any truth in the above, what can be done? The answer, I believe, is mission—a three-pronged mission.

A Three Pronged Mission
Mission to Our Own Minds

We are all intellectual atheists with split minds. In church we confess God as creator and redeemer, and the Trinity as the ultimate fact. In our schools and colleges we study creation but call it nature and ignore the God who made it. We study history and ignore its Lord whom we confess in church. The church's ultimate fact, the Trinity, is not even on our school and college curriculum. So the missions should begin with ourselves really believing (with hearts and soul and strength and mind) what in church we say we believe. That includes believing that the Bible is scripture. In this mental conversion we must prepare for a long haul. At an advanced age I am just beginning.

Mission to the Church

Many parts of the church are partly apostate; the mission, therefore, is a daunting one. Let us begin by asking some questions. Are we still true to our creeds and our traditions? Is the common call to uncertainty a luxury we relish because it is undemanding, but one we cannot afford and scripture prohibits? Is the fear of dogma and creed a camouflage for all the hidden dogmas and hidden creeds of our idolatrous culture? Is liberalism a cover for concealed illiberality, and is uncertainty founded on the destructive certainty that there is no certainty?

Now more positively, can we encourage all ministers to preach the whole council of God, to preach the Bible and not about the Bible? To preach because they have listened to it rather than questioned it? To preach so that congregations are disturbed but do not blame the preacher; rather, they wrestle with scripture because they recognize where the disturbance comes from? To preach the scriptural gospel as true for all men and women in all their activities and not true only for Christians? To preach to enable us all to live in the world but to claim it for Christ? To demonstrate that scripture is public truth and not just private preference?

If we are confessed aliens and eccentrics to the culture, let us be like those early ones in the New Testament—certain that Christ is the truth and willing to be eccentric to the culture for the culture's sake so that it may be redeemed. Many of our forebears used to be proud of their dissent and their nonconformity. We, their descendants, are so conformed to the culture that we are hardly aware of the loss of scripture. Dare we be the new dissenters, not marching under the culture's question mark, but bearing with certainty a cross that both questions and redeems the culture?

Mission to the Culture

One day the kingdoms of this world will become the kingdom of Christ. This is our mission. If we are to recover scripture, the work must go hand in hand with mission to culture, and mission to culture demands the certainty and authority that we possess, from God, only through God's word in scripture.

Consideration of what is meant by mission to culture is not fully defined in this brief statement. However, it is sufficient at present to suggest that recovering scripture is a mission task that is part of the greater whole—mission within and to Western culture.

2

From Canon to Mission

George Herbert, in one of his sonnets on holy scripture, includes these two lines:

> Starres are poore books and oftentimes do misse:
> This book of starres lights to eternall blisse.

At greater length and with infinitely less refinement, I will outline some factors, both positive and negative, that shape my understanding of canon as related to mission.

Canonical Interpretation

The word *canonical*, when used with regard to interpretation, is not intended to be exclusive. It makes room for a variety of forms of interpretation, as long as they in turn do not exclude certain canonical factors. Perhaps all it would exclude would be the subjectivism and selectivism that are the essence of heresy. It is a biblical equivalent of insisting that a reviewer read the whole book and not just the preface and last chapter; that a doctor possess more than a diploma in anatomy; and that a truck driver have more than a motorcycle operator's license.

Canonical interpretation, like some other kinds of interpretation, works with text-immanent exegesis. It cautiously welcomes other kinds, such as structuralism and literary criticism, but does not welcome being identified with them.

By being insistently concerned with the whole canon, it opposes a conscious canon within the canon and seeks to draw attention to the dangers of unconscious canons within the canon.

Although admitting that the concept itself could become a fetish, emphasis on the whole canon provides a means of judging all attempts to discover a validating center. The search for such a center is not excluded. It might even be encouraged if it found a center whose circumference met the canonical criteria. If I were asked to suggest a center, I would suggest Philippians 2:5–11.

One virtue of the canonical emphasis is that it conscientizes biblical users against a merely illustrative use of scripture that passes for something much more significant. The kingdom of God can have fewer, more treasonable offenses than the use of scripture to conceal the nonscriptural. The devil's expertise in this form of deception is well documented.

I understand the canonical hermeneutic as one essentially directed to decision and action and ultimately inseparable from mission. The rationale for this statement is not merely impatience with the theoretical hermeneutic. It emerges from the fact that the whole canon is concerned with the witness to and the movement toward the new heavens and the new earth, and that no understanding of any part of that whole can allow it to escape from its place and therefore its responsibility within the whole movement.

Canonical interpretation is as old as the canonical concept. Did that concept begin with the Book of Deuteronomy? Possibly. But equally, it is very new in at least one major respect. It must now build upon the knowledge and full acceptance of the dynamic diversity within scripture. Perhaps we should be bold and insist that we rejoice and celebrate the new freedom we now have to look upon the many-splendored thing that scripture is. We must acknowledge the tensions, the contradictions, the paradoxes, and the dialectics with which it abounds. We do not pretend they are not there. We do not silence them with a dogma that does not arise from them. We do not camouflage them with the wrong use of allegory or typology, which is not to deny a good use of allegory and typology. They are our raw material that as far as possible must render us the appropriate methods and skills to work with it. We must learn afresh how to hear and to sit astonished in this parliament of voices. We must learn that the government moves from party to party and that the opposition is frequently Her Majesty's loyal opposition, as we say in Great Britain. We must struggle to know which are the true and which are the false prophets, and to believe that in the anger, conflict, and rancorous antiphonies as well as in laws, lyrics, apocalypses, proverbs, oracles, broken myths, and fables, there are the self-modifying and self-rectifying forces that will ultimately enable us to hear the word of the Lord for today. The conscious attempt always to see the part in the light of the whole should bring fresh nuances of meaning to old words. The larger context means that every part is overshadowed by both judgment and mercy, both creation and redemption, both death and life. No part is isolated. No text or chapter or book is an island to itself. All are part of the main, and therefore all in varying degrees point to both goodness and severity, to both piety and politics.

The discipline has much from the church's tradition to build upon, but much will have to be new. Certainly, both old and new will be needed in the vast undertaking of investigating afresh the interpretation of the Old Testament canon that is found in the New Testament, and of learning to hear this in some sense as normative and authoritative for us. If anyone says this is easier said than done, I respond, "Yes, it is." But that applies to the whole of Christian life and is no reason for not attempting it.

From Canon to Mission

This chapter considers the movement from canon to mission. In Chapter 3 we will survey the mission scene in order to discern which questions should be brought from mission to the canon. Although this chapter begins in the canon and not in mission, it is actually concerned with one particular set of questions that arise within mission. They are the questions of confusing diversity. There are many reasons for the lack of consensus within missions and churches about the nature of mission, but one of them already referred to is a form of fragmentation. This fragmentation, even polarization, is a reflection of the fragmentation and atomism that permeate so much understanding of the Bible. Lacking a canonical reading of the Bible, with its inner critiques and self-correcting tensions, the biblical fragments tend to support fragmented mission with all its dangers of imbalance, single-issue fanaticism, and heresy.

With these dangers in mind we turn to the unity of scripture and mission. The modern ecumenical movement saw the rise of the phrase "mission and unity," the word "unity" invariably referring to church unity. One purpose of this book is to extend the connotation and usage of the word "unity" in that phrase. In the present age of theological confusion, it is also necessary to stress, in addition to church unity, the unity of the Trinity and the unity of the Bible. Mission not only turns on and points to a united church; it also depends on trinitarian and biblical unity as, ideally, in the name of the Father, Son, and Holy Spirit, the whole Bible is heard speaking within the whole church to the whole world. Such an ideal is beyond both grasp and reach, but it is within the bounds of our competence to attempt to relate the question of mission to the whole of scripture. Biblical scholarship has long been hesitant to speak of biblical unity, and Christians who have professed it have rarely if ever expressed it adequately in either theory or practice. Is it unfair to suggest that biblical scholarship entered into postmodernity a hundred and fifty years before postmodernism was ever thought of because about a hundred and fifty years ago we reduced the Bible to stories and fragments of stories without the grand metanarrative that gave coherence and meaning to them? We were way ahead of the world. Consequently, we must ask if it is possible today to speak of the Bible as a whole, or are we confined to its pieces? Is it legitimate to break through the analytical mold to a usable synthesis?

Observation on the Word Unity

Our word "Bible" comes from the French *bible* which comes from the Latin word *biblia*. *Biblia* was first read as a neuter plural. Then it was read as a feminine singular. Thus from the beginning there was a proper tension between singularity and plurality, and this tension was well maintained. Up to the eighteenth century it was assumed that the Bible was a mysterious unity greater than its parts. The loss of unity, in a sense, is a fairly recent happening.

Within the last twenty years or so, biblical studies aided by literary criticism have started to produce a change of mood that makes it increasingly easier to speak of unity. The following are just straws in the wind.

1. People like Walter Wink (1973), Eta Linnemann (1990), Jon Levenson (1993), and many others have been critical of some aspects of modern biblical studies with the result that some biblical criticism is now less dogmatic than it was. There is a lot of heart searching now going on in biblical studies.

2. There are more kinds of holistic approach, a recent return to text-immanent exegesis, and a demand for theological commentaries that go beyond the historical-critical type.

3. Some of the foremost literary critics, such as Northrop Frye, Gabriel Josipovici, Frank Kermode, and Yehezkel Kaufmann working with text-immanent exegesis

and defending the canon, have accused biblical scholarship of doing everything but read the Bible. And they have been heard by some biblical scholars.

4. Hermeneutics since Gadamer have made it possible for Paul Ricoeur to speak of the second naiveté and enabled increasing numbers of people to explore the strengths of being naive. Later in this chapter I am going to be very naive. I will take you back to Sunday School.

5. Growing criticism of Enlightenment presuppositions and their effect on biblical studies; epistemological writings, especially those of Michael Polanyi (1958); Y. Kaufmann (1961), George Steiner (1989), Jon Levenson (1993), and other Jewish writers; a new understanding of typology; a recovered sympathy for allegory; and the increasing contributions of Catholic scholarship have helped to change the intellectual climate and loosen the bonds of both liberal and conservative dogmatism.

6. Finally, and most significantly, American scholars from within recognized biblical scholarship, led by Brevard Childs (1974) and J. A. Sanders (1972; 1987), have begun to change attitudes and restore confidence in the canon.

Quite rightly, individuals and churches make statements about social and political issues and claim that they are Christian. Some such statements patently owe more to current ideologies than to the Bible. Some may quote biblical passages; but without a recognized discipline of how the Bible should be used, such quotations give rise to suspicion and questioning. The church is in a dilemma. If Christ is Lord, he is lord of the public sphere and not only lord of believing individuals and of the church. Therefore the church, to whom is committed the witness to that lordship, must speak to the public domain; but if it is to speak with confidence and authority, then, in speaking, the church must know it is speaking out of the whole counsel of God as revealed in scripture and not out of some canon within the canon or some arbitrary principle of selection. In other words, to the best of its ability, the church must speak canonically or forever hold its peace lest in its own self-deception it deceives the very world it would save.

I have tried briefly to show that it is now easier than it was not too long ago to speak of the unity of the Bible. It is easier but not easy. It is still a minority opinion among biblical scholars, and dare any of us claim that we truly practice its use in speaking of public truth? Even if it were a majority opinion in both church and study, would that give us grounds authoritatively to relate the canon to mission? I think not. Our grounds are in faith and not in the ballot box. Our grounds are in the creeds where we confess our faith and we affirm the unity of the Godhead and the oneness of the church. The unity of the scriptures ultimately is also a faith affirmation. Supporting reasons are welcome and aid our public affirmation by providing added plausibility, but proper confidence rests in faith and not in the fashions of reason. Too long we have robbed the church of its proper authority by subjecting biblical norms and standards to norms and standards of a culture that began three centuries ago to replace the light of Christ with other lights, his truth with other truths, his way with other ways, and his life with existence. With our intellects we have known that the plausibility structures of Christendom were long gone and that we already live in a pagan world, but the force of habit is so strong that we have continued to welcome the delusion that the culture still gives support. And, almost unthinkingly, we have allowed it to judge, demote, and demean what, in church, we call the word of God.

In seeking to make the Bible relevant we have robbed it of the power that is the sole reason for making it relevant. We have assumed that relevance meant accommodation. We have permitted a culture, which equally depends on faith-acceptance, to judge the Christian contrast or counterculture that in God's name should be the source of judgment and redemption. Modernity and postmodernity have left the church bereft of that which is also their hope as well as the church's. Consequently, we affirm the Bible's unity by faith because only faith can provide the necessary security and authority. To attempt to provide an anchor in some rational proof would, in fact, be to rely on whatever belief lay behind the proof. Our proper confidence lies in our faith. Armed then with such confidence, we must cease to bring our norm to the bar of alien norms, and with missionary zeal, we must reverse the process, bringing the other norms to judgment and eventually to redemption. A unity that our pre-enlightened forefathers took for granted has to be recovered and relearned.

In the past two hundred years the understanding of unity has changed. We, the believers, certainly have. So how do we relearn and recover? When Paul was struggling with singularity and plurality, he compared the church to a human body. We also can make a beginning by comparing the canon to an individual person. What I am trying to do here, and what follows in this chapter, is to help us reclaim for ourselves or, perhaps for some of us, to begin to acquire canonical literacy in such a way that we overhear the echoes that any one part of the Bible sets tingling in our ears.

The Unity of the Individual

I wish I were like the writer to the Hebrews, who concentrated wholly and single-mindedly on Jesus Christ. He apparently can hear all the echoes from the Old Testament, and he knows how to use them. He is doing a canonical job with, in his day, canonical literacy. A great deal of theology nowadays is written about story and narrative. How do we get hold of that story, especially the big story, the metanarrative? I want to try to do that here. But first, let me say three things about what makes me, as a person, one:

1. My oneness is dynamic and not static. It is a living unity and exists in the midst of growth and change. If I had

never changed, if I had never grown physically, intellectually, emotionally, and morally, you would have said, "He's
not all there!" Unity demands growth and change.

2. The individual understands personal unity through a
mixture of factual observation and faith. I can see the skin-
bound entity that I am. That is visible, but I believe that I
have a mind and a soul and a spirit, and I believe that they
are all interconnected and that all of them together are me,
I hope I am one and not legion.

3. My unity consists of many contributory unities rang-
ing from the unity of the skeleton, the unity of the digestive
system, the unity of the circulatory system, the unity of the
lymphatic glands, and so forth, and plus whatever mental,
emotional, and spiritual unities I possess.

The Dynamic Unity of the Bible

The normal man or woman is a dynamic unity of unities
known by the senses and by faith. The Bible, in its scriptural mode, is also dynamic and new every morning. Its
unity is known factually and also by faith. It is also a unity
that consists of countless contributory unities. I now suggest a few of these contributory unities and thereby cumu-
latively to give glimpses of the total unity with a view to
showing that biblical totalities point clearly in the direction
of mission and the need for mission. Moreover, the more
we reclaim the Bible as a whole, the more we see the
canonical scriptures as providing a missionary mandate, a
mission critique, and a missionary objective. So now, in the
attempt to increase our canonical literacy, let us go to
Sunday School. Before doing so, we must distinguish
between biblical literacy and scriptural literacy. According
to Charles Marson:

> These children can tell you who Huppim and
> Muppim and Ard were; they know the latitude of
> Beersheba, Kerioth and Bethgamal; they can tell you
> who slew a lion in a pit on a snowy day; they have

ripe views upon the identity of Nathaniel and St. Bartholomew; they can name the destructive miracles, the parables peculiar to St. Luke, and, above all, they have a masterly knowledge of St. Paul's second missionary journey. They are well loaded and ballasted with chronicles of Baasha and Zimri, Methuselah and Alexander the Coppersmith.... Therefore while our clergy are... instant in season and out of season... to proclaim the glories of Huppim and Muppim, the people are destroyed for lack of knowledge.... They know all about Abraham except the way to his bosom, all about David except his sure mercies, and all about St. Paul except the faith which he preached and which justified him (quoted in Kenneth Leech 1986:6–7).

Here is biblical literacy with total absence of scriptural literacy. And that speaks critically to me, although I had to look in the concordance for Huppim and Muppim. But they are there.

What I want to do now, quickly and impressionistically, is to look at eight ways of seeing the Bible as a whole. I will say a little more about the latter four or five because each one of these ways of seeing the Bible as a totality includes within it what I have been trying to suggest—that the whole Bible seen as a whole points us to mission. Let us look quickly at some of the other ways.

Ways of Seeing the Bible as a Unity

The first way of seeing the Bible as a whole is the U pattern, an idea that comes from Northrop Frye. You begin in glory and you end in glory, but there is the descent and the ascent. The whole Bible fits into this pattern. You begin with the creation and God sees it is good; you move through the loss of Israel, the death of Jesus Christ, and you end up in the new creation—from glory unto glory.

This is the pattern of the whole of scripture; you find that pattern almost wherever you look. Consider: the one from Philippians, the *kenosis* hymn already mentioned above: six verses beautifully balanced, the first three the descent, the next three the ascent. I believe almost wherever you look in scripture you will find that U pattern, the pattern from glory unto glory. The Bible moves from creation to new creation, and it moves from creation to new creation via all the sendings—the sending of Abraham, the sending of Israel, the sending of Christ, the sending of the church, through all the sendings and testimonies.

Second, the Bible can be seen as a unity in terms of types and antitypes—the Old Testament types and then the antitypes in the New Testament. It can be seen as a tale of promise and fulfillment, the whole leaning forward until the coming of Christ; and then the continued leaning forward to the new Jerusalem and the new heavens and the new earth. Some people have seen the Bible in terms of the four great words: the word to Abraham, the word to Moses, the word to David, the word to Jesus. And then another way of seeing it is to see how virtually all the themes in the Old Testament eventually focus on Jesus Christ. It is easy to work backward to see that almost every major Old Testament theme is applied to Jesus Christ. He is the Messiah; he is prophet, priest, and king. It is a kind of isosceles triangle. The Bible arranges that the themes in the Old Testament point to Jesus Christ.

The third way of seeing the Bible is the model of the Old Testament and the New Testament as torso and head: the Old Testament incomplete; the Old Testament in a sense a failure; the New Testament incomprehensible without the Old; the two belonging together, and the Old Testament in a sense being a creation of the New Testament. One thing that fascinates me is the interdependence of the two Testaments. It is the historical truth and the witness of the Old Testament that enables the apostles to preach the gospel, and yet at the same time the Old Testament would not exist if it were not for the New Testament. And in taking over what we call the Old Testament, the Old Testament as the "Hebrew scriptures" is partially destroyed because the so-called integrity of the Old Testament, which I as a teacher proclaimed for many years, really finds its true integrity joined with the New Testament. That integrity, of course, is Jesus Christ. Christians, when they took over the Hebrew scriptures to make them into the Old Testament, did something revolutionary. They took out the center part of the Hebrew scriptures and put it at the end. The prophets were taken from the middle, from between the Torah and the writings, and put at the end because the prophets were read in the church as prophecies of Jesus Christ and so would have to be put nearest the Gospels. So we have our Old Testament ending with the forward-looking conclusion of Malachi, and then you come immediately to the Gospels and the coming of Jesus Christ.

Fourth, the Bible is seen as moving from a beginning to an end. Here I'm beginning to move toward those ways of understanding scripture that imply that the whole of scripture is a mission. You move in the Bible from a rural Eden to an urban Eden. Scripture begins with a terrible warning about gardens. They are dangerous places, and the movement in the Bible through a whole series of cities is to the urban Eden in Jerusalem. And what happens in that new Jerusalem? Who goes into the new Jerusalem? After the terrifying cleansing and purifying by the blood shedding in Revelation, all tribes and tongues and peoples go into the new Jerusalem. Here is the acceptance of the whole progress of civilization. In a sense, this is the "yes" to our civilizations, to our endeavors, centered so much as they are on sinful cities. The ambiguity of the city is shown to us right from the beginning because the first city was built by Cain. Cain was under the mark of grace, but he was the murderer. Here we see what cities are. But finally, the civ-ilizations, the cultures, of all tribes and tongues and people are received into the new Jerusalem. There has been a mighty mission work going along through the whole tale in order to move from that rural Eden to the urban Eden.

A fifth way of looking at scripture is to see the Bible as a series of variations on five themes, five relationships, that are enunciated right in the beginning of the Old Testament.

a. *The relationship between God and creation.* "In the beginning God created the heavens and the earth" (Gen. 1:1).

b. *The relationship between God and humanity.* Call it the religious relationship if you like (Gen. 1:26–27).

c. *The relationship between persons.* Call it the social or the political relationship, beginning with the most important of those human relationships—that between man and woman. That relationship is so important that it is enunciated in two different ways, in the "P" account and in the "J" account (Gen. 1:26–27; 2:18–24).

d. *The relationship between humankind and cre-ation.* This too is enunciated in different ways. Man/woman is made in the image of God in order that he/she may be able to be the steward of creation. In Genesis 2 man names the animals. There is a very close relationship between humankind and creation, the eco-logical relationship.

e. *The relationship of the individual to oneself.* Man/woman is a self-knowing being. This is the psycho-logical relationship.

These themes are enunciated, and in short order they are all distorted. By the end of Genesis 3 all these themes have been distorted, even the relationship between God and creation, because God has cursed creation. Then we ask, "What really is the work of Jesus Christ? If we take the New Testament as a whole seriously, is Christ's work limited to saving the individual or saving the church? Is not Christ's work the restoring of these five relationships?" The problem begins with the second relationship. It is in the religious relationship where things go wrong in the Old Testament: the relationship between God and man/woman goes wrong, and the other four relationships very quickly are distorted.

The healing of that relationship through the work of Jesus Christ also begins with the human being reconciled to God. The reconciliation of humankind to God begins the healing of the other four relationships. In Jesus Christ there is neither male nor female, neither bond nor free. In the New Testament salvation is best understood if it is seen as the healing of these five relationships.

When I went to Taiwan in 1950 from mainland China, the first summer conference was addressed by the Taiwanese general secretary of the Presbyterian Church of Taiwan. He spoke on "The Work of Christ: Repairing a Broken Universe." This way of looking at the unity of scripture—the five broken relationships and the healing in Christ—gives us a wonderful introduction to what mission is, and this understanding of the Bible provides a strong critique of our polarization in mission.

If the work of Christ is to heal these five relationships, we can never be satisfied with our narrow, selective definitions of salvation. Such an understanding puts priority on preaching because it is the preaching that brings about confession, forgiveness, and salvation of the believer. Those who base their mission entirely on Matthew 28 have the right priority. The trouble is that often they stop at that relationship. On the other hand, mission activists are also shown that they do not begin in the right place. They begin by trying to solve the world's problems. Thus there is a critique of the so-called evangelical approach and a critique of the activist or developmental missionary. And so you get a standard for judging views of salvation and for judging how the work is done.

A sixth way of trying to see the unity of scripture is through the series of promises, blessings, and covenants in Genesis 1–11 that precede Abraham. There are covenants with Noah, implied covenants with Adam. God promises not to destroy the earth again. Promises, blessings, and covenants—in Genesis 1–11 these are indiscriminate and impersonal. These require no testimony, no faith. They require no response, no obedience. With Abraham a change is introduced. God makes more promises and blessings and covenants, but these are discriminate. You do not know about these unless you are told. These demand witness, testimony. They demand faith and obedience. The Bible presents to us these two ranges of blessing, promise, and covenant. The one range provides us with stability, continuity, and security; the other provides us with redemption. The first range does not need to be proclaimed or accepted in faith. The second requires the response of testimony, witness, and faith. In a sense, the whole Bible is a dialogue—a missionary dialogue—between these two activities of God.

There is a seventh pattern, also of grace to grace or of glory to glory, which we see introduced in the earliest chapters in Genesis. Adam and Eve are given everything that is necessary to live. They sin and are punished, but that is not the end. God shows them grace. They are not killed, and death is presented as a mercy; because if you have sinned, to live forever would be frightening. In the story of the next generation, Cain and Abel were given all that is necessary, but they too sinned. Cain sins and is punished, but there is grace. He gets the mark of grace. Then Genesis tells the flood story. The terrifying sin in the flood story is followed by punishment and then the almost overwhelming mercy at the end of the flood story. You become accustomed to the pattern of grace, sin, forgiveness, grace. The tower of Babel story seems to have the same ingredients: sin, punishment—but no grace. Grace comes in the call of Abraham. The rest of the Bible becomes the answer to the tower of Babel. Finally, the breakdown at Babel is restored with the coming of the Spirit in Acts 2.

Eighth, and last, consider the fourfold promise to Abraham: he would become a great people, God would be with him, he would possess the land, he would be blessed and through him the nations of the world would be blessed.

At this point I want to use my imagination. These four promises to Abraham might be seen as the formation of the first missionary society. Abraham was called to be a blessing to the nations; but if he was going to do that, he had to have certain things: a people, the accompaniment of God, and the resources that only the land could provide. These promises provide the missionary society with its resources. The first takes us right through the whole of the Book of Genesis. Read the Book of Genesis asking yourself, "Will Abraham ever be a great people?" To be a great people he has to have a son. You soon begin to wonder, "What kind of God is this? Why on earth did he choose this man Abraham?" Because in the second part of chapter 12, after being called, Abraham shows himself to be father of the unfaithful as much as of the faithful. Pharaoh is shown to be more of a gentleman than Abraham. Why did God do this? Immediately the promise is put in jeopardy. If Sarai had gone into the harem of the Pharaoh, what would have happened to the promise? Right through Genesis God seems to be planting thorns in his own footsteps. Finally, the baby arrives, and it's such an amazing thing that Sarai christens him Isaac, which might be translated "What a hoot!" The baby arrives, and then God says, "Sacrifice him." Will the promise be kept? Of course it isn't really kept, because by the end of Genesis there are only seventy people.

When is the promise kept? It is kept at the beginning of Exodus. The promise in Exodus is that they are too numerous.

Genesis is linked to Exodus. Along with Leviticus, Exodus is concerned with the problem "Will God be with us?" Again you've got your heart in your throat. Is God going to be with them? Will the covenant be made? You go through the ten plagues, and God's promise is threatened. Finally, in Exodus 19 the covenant is offered. The inauguration ceremony of the covenant occurs in Exodus 24. Ah! We're home and dry. Thereupon Aaron, typical of many priests and ministers perhaps, falls into idolatry and the whole thing begins over again. Afterward God is really angry and the covenant is being remade; but it has got to be kept. Five chapters are devoted to plans for building the tabernacle. This is absolutely disproportionate unless you see it as "How the relationship with God is preserved."

Then you come to Leviticus. The tabernacle is built, but what do you do in the tabernacle? What kind of worship and ritual is needed to keep God with you? That takes you right through Leviticus.

Numbers and Deuteronomy are dominated by the promise of the land. Numbers has little to do with numbers (the Hebrew means "in the wilderness"). Will the people ever get to the promised land? Again you feel the tension as you read through Numbers.

Finally, Deuteronomy. How do you keep the land once you occupy it? How do you maintain the land? That takes you through the book, but you get no final solution. You have to wait until Joshua before the land is claimed. The Pentateuch is joined to the former prophets by that third promise.

What about the fourth promise? Of course, the fourth promise is of blessing to the nations; and that is a promise, in a sense, that keeps you on the edge of your chair right through the rest of the Old Testament. Will Israel, the descendants of Abraham, be a light and blessing to the nations? That joins the Old Testament to the New, because throughout the Old Testament you have to wait expectantly—as Jews waited—for the coming of Jesus Christ, the true light and blessing to the nations.

Finally, you can see the whole of the Bible as a five-act drama. First act: Genesis 1–11, the problem. The viceroy has mutinied and creation is threatened. Second act: Genesis 12 to Malachi, the beginning of mission, the first sending. The king sends Israel. Third act: the four Gospels. The king sends his Son, the true Israel. Fourth act: Acts to Revelation 20. The Son sends the Spirit into the church, the new Israel, to announce God's reign. Fifth act: Revelation 21–22 no problem, re-creation, the new heavens and the new earth. All this is done by the succession of sending and those sent. The new heavens and new earth are achieved through this continuing sending and the continuing testimony.

Forgive me the shorthand and impressionistic presentation. It is a long time since I taught Sunday School. I can only hope that I may have provoked you to explore the countless ways in which scripture can be seen as a unity and to ask whether this unity is a unity in the service of mission.

3

From Mission to Canon

Mission emerges from the canon, and its aims and objectives and motives are determined by the canon. It is to the canon that we must turn when questions arise out of the work of mission. In chapters 3 and 4 we will bring questions from and concerning mission to the canon. In this chapter we will first briefly survey today's missionary scene for the purpose of identifying some of the major questions and controversies in mission today. (George A. Lindbeck [1989] has observed that as we lose scripture, our culture loses imaginative potential for artistic expression.) I do this not in the belief that the canon is the ultimate court of appeal. That is the heavenly court before the throne of God. But I believe that the canon is a better context in which to pass judgment than the limited ideological, cultural, historical, and biblical fragmentary contexts we often employ; and, at most, it is the best we have this side of heaven if we learn to use it aright. In chapter 4, I will follow the same path but restrict myself to one issue that can be examined in greater detail while using it to demonstrate a somewhat different method of approach.

On the European scene it has become almost a cliché to say, with Walter Freytag, that mission once had problems but has now itself become the problem. This is demonstrated by the declining interest in most European churches, reduced financial support, the growing conviction that the long-established missionary societies are in crisis, that missionary training is unsure of its role, and that mission is a form of imperialism about which we should be apologetic. The evidence is all too clear. Add to this the church's homegrown mission against mission led by John Hick, Wilfred Cantwell Smith, Paul Knitter, and others. Further proof of the general malaise is offered by particular problems, of which I offer a selection.

1. Mission tends to polarize into conservative versus liberal, conciliar versus evangelical, action versus proclamation, development versus conversion, church versus kingdom, social justice versus individual piety, and political liberation versus personal liberation from sin. The list is endless.

2. The polarization is frequently associated with biblical fragmentation as the various poles find justification in their own canon within the canon. On occasion this canon is little more than one text and its near relations.

3. We then have the problem of the privileged text, of which the clearest example is the Exodus text used by some liberation theologians. Along with the privileged texts are the privileged words and the privileged vocabulary that tend to act like a talisman.

4. Greater travel, greater pluralism, perhaps in some cases greater understanding and sympathy—all have helped to complicate matters. Most Christians are confused, but a sizable minority have adopted a new "orthodoxy" of compassion, believing that it is wrong to witness to members of other religions; most of all, mission to the Jew is out of the question.

5. The relationship with culture has at least two areas of questioning. In the Two-Thirds World, the problem still is one of contextualization or inculturation. How can Christianity, the Western import, be indigenized and appear homegrown? In old Christendom and wherever Western culture has spread, the problem is how to deal with the acids of modernity and the confusion of postmodernity.

What is it in Western culture that dissolves Christianity and is gospel-resistant? How can we preach Christ, the Savior of the world, in a world increasingly built on cultural assumptions that deny everything essential to belief in Christ?

6. In some missionary activity, the emphasis on the virtues of sharing, partnership, dialogue, justice, bias to the poor, and so forth gives rise to questions as to whether significant expressions of the gospel are not in danger of moving into the center and becoming substitute gospels.

7. Some see mission as discerning what God is doing and cooperating in God's action. Under the cloak of humility, is this the supreme arrogance, in that we appoint ourselves as prophets? How do we know what God is doing? If we do appoint ourselves as prophets, we are inevitably false prophets. I do not presume to know what God is doing. I know what God has done, for the Bible tells me so.

8. In what sense do we let the world set the agenda, and, if we do let the world set the agenda, is there any way of preventing it from writing the minutes?

9. In what sense does mission consist in meeting the world's need, and can we ever know what that need really is unless our analysis begins in the Christian revelation? Can Christ ever be the answer to a question unless he is first the question? E. P. Sanders said that Paul always has the solution before he knows the plight. A book was published in England not long ago called *All You Love Is Need,* showing how need is becoming a subtle kind of idolatry. Can culture be converted? Does scripture have a place for the concepts of atheism and secularism, or are secularism, atheism, agnosticism, and materialism merely camouflages for idolatry? Like the early church in Acts 6, are we in danger of allowing the diaconate to obscure and take over the apostolate? I find Acts 6 very relevant. Why is the "Macedonian" model, which permits mission only on invitation, given such prominence? Has the tendency been since Friedrich D.E. Schleiermacher for theology to

become a kind of anthropology-affected mission? How do we respond to mission as humanization? When mission degenerates into breast beating because of its relation to imperialism, can this readily become a subtle form of postimperial imperialism by suggesting that our confessions of elitism and racial superiority, our reduced consumption, and our changed economics can solve all the Third World problems? Denied the right to proclaim salvation in Christ by feeble theologies, do we unconsciously present ourselves as the source of salvation? The nineteenth-century missionaries almost forgot the doctrine of creation. They went into deepest and remotest Africa and Asia, oblivious of God's presence. In reaction, has the twentieth century tended to lose the doctrine of redemption in the attempt to give rightful place to God the Creator? In the latter part of the twentieth century how are we to interpret and proclaim whatever truth there is in *extra ecclesiam nulla salus*? It seems to me that a theological task of every generation is to relearn the truth in "there is no salvation outside the church." What do we do about the black Christs and the feminist Christs and all the other Christs? And what do we do with an Asian theology that sees divinity in Asianism but not uniquely in that Asian born of an Asian woman whom the Westerners have always proclaimed as God incarnate?

The above list does not presume to be in any way comprehensive, nor do I think that a canonical hermeneutic can easily resolve all these issues and leave us without problems. What I do maintain is that the situation is much worse than it need be because we possess and interpret fragments of scripture instead of a canonical scripture. But any improvement will be difficult unless we recover scripture. When we do recover it and better understand how it functions canonically in the present era, we could be poised for a great missionary advance.

The Canon and Mission to Culture

I want to identify two questions arising from bringing mission to the canon. The first: can we find a canonical way of doing mission to culture? I have been speaking of "mission to culture." If we say that previously we have had mission to individuals, mission to communities and to societies, mission to culture is a new kind of mission. This is mission to the deep, underlying presuppositions and the infrastructures of society rather than the superstructures. Does the Bible give us any guidance as to content and method? Does the Bible provide maps as well as marching orders? Let me offer a brief response that I hope is at least partially canonical. Gerhard Von Rad assured us that scripture records a history created by the word of God; but if so, this history is also the result of a dialogue between God's word and innumerable cultures in countless places over a period of more than two thousand years. Almost every book of both Testaments can be seen to emerge from such a dialogue. If the scripture with its demand for mission to culture is itself the true witness to the true God in, by, through, against, and in behalf of culture, then can scripture be seen to provide method and norm for our mission to culture? Let us take a quick trip through the two Testaments.

Genesis 1, probably emerging first in Babylon, is written against the background of Near Eastern mythology as represented by the Enuma Elish and other creation myths. The myths are invoked in order that they may be repudiated and transformed. They provide categories and vocabulary and act as a foil for the new and true account. Genesis 6–9, the flood story, is written in dialogue with and partial dependence on other ancient Near Eastern traditions as represented primarily by the Gilgamesh epic. Again, there is the invoking and partial dependence only in order to revoke and to affirm a very different understanding of the unruly waters and their purpose. In Exodus,

Israel emerges from the womb of Egyptian culture led by a man who, though Hebrew, could be mistaken for an Egyptian aristocrat. His brother, in the dialogue with idolatry, is seduced and provides succeeding generations with the paradigm of the compromised priest. Deuteronomy warns against the culture. Judges provides a series of largely martial dialogues with a variety of nations in which the tribes vacillate between obedience and disobedience. Prophecy flourishes within the changing hegemonies of imperial overlords: Syria, Assyria, Babylon, and Persia. And the interchange between the chosen people and those on whose behalf they are chosen is clearly apparent. Jeremiah is the only prophet actually appointed to the nations, but the Assyrian presence is clearly discernible in Isaiah, and Babylon's in Ezekiel. Jonah is perhaps to be seen at odds with contemporary Israelite culture in the superior and condemnatory presence of contemporary culture as seen in the seafarers and in the Ninevites. Hosea speaks to an Israel immersed and almost drowned in contemporary Canaanite culture. The Book of Hosea is our contemporary. Hosea's diatribe takes the form of intensive borrowing from that culture in order to oppose it. He borrows the concept of a closed economic system that has no place for Yahweh but maintains that it is the baals who are locked out of Yahweh's system. In combating the concept of sexuality in the Godhead, his boldness exceeds all bounds when he claims that God has a wife who is Israel.

In the New Testament the story is the same. The wedding feast at Cana, our Lord's dialogues with Pilate, the Samaritan woman, and the Syrophoenician woman are obvious examples of what is everywhere present. Under the rule of Rome and firmly within the Hellenic world, the New Testament writers narrate a multifaceted dialogue between Christ and his church, on the one hand, and contemporary culture, on the other; and they narrate it in Greek. Does the census determine the date of Jesus' birth, or does

Micah's prophecy of the birth determine the timing of Caesar Augustus's edict? John 1 turns on the Greek concept of "logos." The Emmaus disciples are blinded by a contemporary form of liberation theology, Stephen enters into controversy with contemporary hermeneutics, Peter dialogues with Cornelius, and Paul confronts the Ephesians. The writer to the Hebrews draws extensively on Jewish interpretations of the past and Platonic understanding of the present. The occasion for Colossians is Gnostic infiltration; and in Revelation, by means of an extensive dialogue with Roman culture, St. John the divine prepares for all tongues and tribes and peoples to enter the New Jerusalem. Such are merely straws, but they are sufficient to indicate the size of their source and the strength of the wind that blows them. The meeting of the Word and culture is indisputable. What does it say to us? We note five points.

1. The ubiquitous encounters between them affirm that the Word is inseparable from the culture. The Word always comes in cultural packages.

2. But the Word is not the packing. Originally inseparable, the Word soon shows its distinctiveness, even its disruptiveness, as it tears apart the packing.

3. The tearing is temporary. Much of the wrapping is recycled. The Word judges but then redeems; it uproots and replants.

4. The pattern everywhere in this process is the pattern of death and resurrection. The gospel of the cross and risen Lord is therefore the main clue to the canonical hermeneutic.

5. All life, public and private, sacred and profane, may be an occasion for mission.

So far, I have attempted to point in one direction where the canon can help us in this amazing task of redeeming our culture, culture that is so powerful and has so imposed itself upon our own minds that we are not aware of our imprisonment within it.

Exodus Within the Canon

The second question centers around how the Exodus functions. The Exodus is one of the main themes in the Bible, and it is one of the most powerful forces for change that the world has ever seen. The ordeal in South Africa, particularly the years 1957–1991, was a struggle between two understandings of the Exodus. The whites had their understanding of the Exodus, and the Pharaohs were the British. The blacks had their understanding of the Exodus, and the Pharaohs were the Dutch. It was a conflict between two interpretations of the Exodus. The power of the Exodus is everywhere. In liberation theology, particularly in Latin America, we know of its great power, but not only there. Almost wherever there is oppression and wherever there is Christian conviction, the Exodus comes to the fore.

My personal wrestle with the Exodus has been long and continuous. It has raised with me many questions concerning the understanding of the canon. By 1971 I had been in Taiwan more than twenty years. My main job was teaching Old Testament. I had not realized that teaching the Old Testament in situations like Taiwan could be a dangerous occupation. In 1971, crisis was in the air. Two things were about to happen. President Nixon was going to see Mao Tse-tung in China, and nobody particularly trusted either of them. The Taiwan government had its reasons to be concerned, and the populace had entirely different reasons. Moreover, the United Nations was to have its annual vote on who ruled China. In retrospect it seems incredible; but until 1970 the Nationalists in Taiwan had always been declared the rightful government of China. Everybody knew in 1971 that the vote would go against Taiwan, and so there was a mood of concern, a mood of anxiety.

In the autumn of 1971 the Nationalists finally lost their United Nations seat to the People's Republic, and President Nixon, hitherto a firm supporter of the Nationalists, visited China and ate, drank, and was merry with Mao Tse-tung. The effects in Taiwan were uncertainty, apprehension, and fear. The government had lost face and diplomatic status. It was confronted with the possibility of American withdrawal should Nixon recognize Peking rather than Taipei. The population cared little about lost face, but they feared greatly Taiwan's absorption into communist China. Much as they resented the Nationalists and longed to be free of their yoke, the Taiwanese did not want to exchange it for what was seen to be a much more grievous one. The known devil in the frying pan is to be preferred to the unknown fire. The dismay and consternation were not lessened by the realization that in all the talking about Taiwan the only people not consulted were the Taiwanese.

Dispirited by fifty years of Japanese colonialism, cowed by the brutal suppression of the 1947 revolt and the succeeding jackboot years, the Taiwanese evidenced little chance of an uprising. This added to their fretting and made it all the more necessary that if a bloodied world was not to see more blood it should hear a voice. There arose a mood—little more—in which men and women wondered if, even in a police state, it were not possible for the majority to address those beyond its borders. Could not someone tell a careless world that the government spoke only for itself, that Peking's talk of liberation was heard as a threat of bondage, and that the vast majority who were already paying the piper wanted to call the tune? Student groups made tentative attempts to make pronouncements, but after twenty years of martial law there was little spirit, little room for maneuver. Even the most genuine and liberal gesture could be seen as yet another government trick.

Finally, after an abortive attempt by an ecumenical group, one church issued a statement. Successfully muzzled on the island itself, copies had been conveyed to governments, churches, and men of influence abroad; and they were able to read what the church had to say. It claimed to be speaking for almost all the people when it asked for two things. First, that in the spirit of the United Nations charter and consistent with the example of numbers of other postcolonial countries, the inhabitants should be allowed to determine their own future. Second, that the Nationalist government should hold general elections.

Read in the West, the statement appeared bland and innocuous, even bathetic. In Taiwan, the land of informers and no *habeas corpus*, where the church had never before entered the political arena, it was an act of supreme courage. It was not done easily or hurriedly. Seldom can an act have been less foolhardy; and no adverse repercussions could ever have matched those imagined. It was true courage because it was done with fear and trembling. Many Taiwanese and Chinese men and women contributed to the making of the statement, and I was privileged to be with some of them as they struggled with their fears, their pasts, their duties, and their God. We were a community of teachers and students in a theological college; and whatever that community contributed of content, courage, and decision to the statement arose in large part from a conscious wrestling with certain passages and themes of the Bible. It is now impossible to list all of them, but three remain with me. In each case I attempt to recapture a little of the dialogue as I heard it; and I can vouchsafe for the fact that men and women did what they would not have thought of doing and did what they least wanted to do, in large part, because they were directly constrained by the Bible. Of the three passages I will choose the Exodus. Only some years later did I became fully aware of the part that the Exodus had played in the African-Americans' fight for equality.

For us in the college, the influence of the book was largely accidental. Every morning at eight o'clock there was worship, with preaching centering around a passage of scripture that was determined by a lectionary adopted some years before. As the autumn term of 1971 commenced, we found ourselves listening to the Book of Exodus. By the third morning we were all conscious that something unprecedented was happening, for as the lesson was read and the sermon delivered, we were thrust out of the chapel into the Exodus happenings that were at one and the same time the threatened oppression and longing for freedom that characterized Taiwan. In defiance of logic and chronology, the two sets of circumstances entered into dialogue and dance. They conversed and influenced each other, first one leading, then the other—at times one pirouetting so that the other was obscured. There was interchange and mutual illumination. Sometimes the differences screamed at us. At times the two became one. We were both outside the dance, whether watching or promoting was not clear, and partners in it. We locked arms with Moses and became men of valor in Taiwan; we murmured with Israel and followed the fainthearted chorus of some of our contemporaries, including the majority of the missionaries.

For those of us who were called to preach on these mornings, it was a new experience. In some ways it was intolerably hard, a thing to be avoided—not because you did not know what to say; you knew precisely what you should say. The hardship was in finding the courage to say it. Sermons wrote themselves, but they didn't preach themselves; and some were prepared that were never delivered. We who were "professionals," paid to read and expound scripture, were coming to this book of the Bible as though for the first time; and both Pharaoh and Moses acquired a distinctly Chinese look. Identities seemed to be interchangeable. Modern names were given to ancient men. Pharaoh's host encamped about us, and the taskmasters carried revolvers. We saw Moses in every show of Taiwanese tenacity, and Israel walked in our cowardice. We knew Exodus better than the scholars because we were there. We saw Taiwan's predicament better than did the politicians because it was illuminated by divine commentary. A religious book became more "religious" because its profoundly secular and political nature was revealed by the prism of Taiwan, and the limitless concern of God with the whole creation became apparent. Inevitably, our identification was with the Hebrews, sometimes with Moses in his boldness, often with Israel's timidity. This was aided by the realization that God's involvement was by no means so simple and so unilateral. The character of Pharaoh's daughter did not permit us to see all Egyptians as bad and Pharaoh's own obduracy as excuse inasmuch as it was God who hardened his heart. The two national identities became intertwined, a mutual interdependence. Although God was clearly with his people, God could also be discerned walking in the enemy camp.

Men and women brought up in the church with the tradition of piety rather than prophetism were not accustomed to what they were hearing. In a country where trade unions were merely part of the apparatus of oppression, it was not easy to see Moses' role when leaders of the bricklayers' union engaged in a walkout. With reluctance the people saw that Moses, the great religious lawgiver, also had political and military responsibility, and that as the "Israel of God" following one "greater than Moses," the church itself might on occasion be called to a similar duty. The odd irreligious methods used in the service of religious freedom puzzled but instructed. What is stranger than the plagues? Blood may have an established place in most revolutionary handbooks, but frogs? And what of the death of the first-born? Dare we contemplate the possibility that this classical bid for freedom was successful because God assumed the role of assassin? All this of course is the merest fraction of a total experience, much of it unexpressed at the time even in corners and whispers. Moreover, it is as one man remembers it, and he a partial outsider and foreigner. We should be cautious with our conclusions yet still keeping in the forefront of our minds the simple fact that some hesitant Christians were moved reluctantly to decision and action partly through an encounter with this book of the Bible.

In asking how people use the Bible, this sort of activity is part of our raw material for investigation; and eventually we either legitimate what was done, having made recommendations for improvement, or we say that this has been tried and found wanting. Therefore, expunge it from the church's life. I am sure that my colleagues in Taiwan would agree that in this meeting with the Bible we were granted ghostly gifts of courage, faith, devotion, and willpower—but that was not all. In the package of grace was specific knowledge that led to decision.

I have continued to struggle with what we did. Did we do the right thing? With one part of my mind I have no doubt whatsoever. We were motivated by the Bible to act. But intellectually I have many questions.

The Exodus, with its attendant themes of Passover, covenant making, the wilderness wandering, and the promise of the land, is central to the Old Testament and never far away in the New Testament. Its shadow is there in Mark 1 and in the baptism and temptation of Jesus. It is still influentially there in the Book of Revelation, especially chapter 15. Its influence has been felt in many periods of church history, and not least in the present period when its power is felt in countless situations where Christians are compelled to struggle against injustice and for liberation. Moses is present whenever people sing "We shall overcome" and "Let my people go." That the model of the Exodus functions powerfully is not in doubt.

How it functions is less clear, and whether it functions as it ought to is a matter for debate. The debate is not new. Perhaps it is present in the Exodus narrative itself. Undoubtedly, Israel was freed from Pharaoh's oppression.

Liberation of a physical and political nature occurred, but why and how did it occur? The occasion was the cry of a people in distress, but motive and method are not simple. Moses is not a single-minded liberation leader. Freedom is hardly mentioned. Moses is a most reluctant cooperator with God. Frequently, the liberated Israelites opt for oppression rather than freedom. On the one occasion when Moses murdered an oppressor as a liberator might be expected to, he was totally unsuccessful if revolution was his intention. Furthermore, the main motive appears to be not a strong desire for freedom but to prove that God hears prayer, that God is the liberator, and the assassin if necessary, that humans must not take matters into their own hands, and that the real purpose is that the people shall worship God in the desert, make a covenant at Sinai, and inherit the promised land—all this, moreover, to fulfill the promises made earlier to the patriarchs. A good case can be made for seeing the narrative as opposed to the suggestion that humans can free themselves; rather, God is a merciful God who hears prayer, hates oppression, and is mighty to save. The human contribution is the very opposite of political activism. Man/woman is expected to cry out, to trust, and eventually to make covenant and to keep covenant. The debate continues throughout the Old Testament. Here are two examples.

The attitude adopted by Jeremiah, particularly in chapter 29, has no place for the people of Judah to oppose oppression because it is of God. God sends the oppression and does not even advocate hoping for liberation. That expectation belongs to the false prophets. The second example is found in Second Isaiah. Isaiah, it is true, looks for political liberation, among other things, and his work is so saturated with the Exodus image that he sees the future hope as a second Exodus, but still the debate continues. The exiles are no more expected to take initiative than was Moses. The comforting and redeeming God will do it all.

Israel's time of service is ended, and they have already suffered twice as much as they should have. The highlight of
this particular debate, and perhaps the soundest clue to
our questions to be found in the Old Testament, is in Isaiah
43:14ff. Two verses in that passage refer to the Exodus.
They look back to the Exodus; but then, speaking like a
1968 hippie, Second Isaiah says, "Forget the past. God is
doing a new thing." Don't trust anyone over thirty! But
then he goes on to describe the new Exodus, and the new
Exodus is in the pattern of the old. What exactly is he saying as he both rejects the Exodus and approves it?

Consider Jesus' mission and the Exodus. Was Jesus cir-
cumscribed and hindered by views of the Exodus that
would have distorted his mission? If so, how did he
respond? In what way, or ways, was the Exodus present in
the consciousness of Jesus? A sketch will have to suffice. In
commenting on Luke 4:21 and 24:27, 44, George Caird
(1963) says, "These last two passages further assert that
Jesus fulfilled, not just a few isolated promises made by the
prophets but the whole tenor, purport, and pattern of Old
Testament teaching and history. In particular he fulfilled the
Exodus and the Passover" (:34). The Exodus thus provided
a model and framework for his whole ministry and mission,
and, surprisingly, within this framework there are many references, allusions, and pointers to the Exodus. Jesus' baptism and emerging from the water, his commissioning and
consequent temptation in the wilderness have all been seen
as recapitulation of Exodus motifs. Particularly, Matthew
shows him as the new Moses. The Last Supper in Luke is
presented as a transformed Passover. Jesus' mission in Luke
4 is described in terms from Isaiah 61 that reflect the first
Exodus. In Luke 9:31, his death is referred to as his exodus.
The Exodus is all about us in the Gospels as it is in the
Epistles and in Revelation.

Assuming then the presence of the Exodus motifs, what
interpretations of them were present, and was there conflict

with Christ's own understanding? Contemporary Jewish understandings stressed the aspect of freedom. Brevard Childs sums it up by saying that "the exodus was above all the formation of a nation of freed men who had been set free from oppression. It was this understanding that lay behind the expectation of the disciples. At least one of them was a zealot who was committed to the struggle for liberation and perhaps all of them had expectations of the kingdom which Jesus preached that were greatly colored by hopes and longings that reached back to the time of Moses. Mention of the kingdom in Acts 1:3 produced the words in verse 6, Lord, will you at this time restore the kingdom to Israel? The same hope that Jesus would restore national independence also appears in Luke 24:21 and no doubt lies behind such political aspirations as are found in Mark 10:35 and Luke 22:24. Thus the Exodus motifs and the contemporary liberation interpretation are both present in the New Testament" (Childs 1974:232). But does the Exodus motif occur with new and alternative understandings? Childs comments, "It is a striking fact how seldom in the New Testament this unbroken identification with the Exodus occurs" (:233) and then goes on to suggest three ways in which the older understandings are changed.

First, it is characteristic of the New Testament to place the redemption out of Egypt into a new context that radically alters its meaning and function for early Christianity (Matt. 2:15). Jesus is the true redeemer of Israel.

Second, it is characteristic of the New Testament to shift the emphasis away from the first Exodus to the second (Luke 3:4ff.).

The third characteristic is to deny that the Exodus gave Israel freedom (Acts 13) or salvation (1 Cor. 10:11ff.; Hebrews 8) and to assert that the goals of the Exodus were reached only in Christ (:232–33).

Jesus' View of the Exodus Model

In all this, where does Jesus himself stand? In Acts 1:6ff.,
Jesus' answer is not a direct "No" but a new direction and
the promise of a power far greater than politics would provide. In Luke 24:25 he rectifies the "liberation" interpretation offered by the other disciples, and by expounding all
the law and the prophets—his whole canon—he makes
them point to his death and resurrection. Is it possible that
the Temptation itself has to be interpreted as strong resistance to the pressures of the Exodus model? It is in a setting that includes other Exodus motifs (noted above), and
it is in a wilderness and lasts forty days and nights, which
might be reminiscent of Israel's forty years of desperation
and temptation. The three great themes of Christ's temptation recapitulate Exodus themes: the miraculous provision
of bread; the overwhelming miracle that stills opposition;
and the surrender of political authority by an evil power
and the freedom to exercise that authority for good. The
temptations are each vanquished by Mosaic words from
Deuteronomy, which was then assumed to come from the
Exodus period. Could this imply that Christ's greatest and
ongoing struggle was with understandings of salvation that
were greatly influenced by traditional interpretations of
the Exodus event and that these were not only external
temptations but were at the same time internal? So he
regarded them as real temptations and resisted them. But
was the resistance total? Did he spiritualize the Exodus?
Did he always interpret it in terms of his death, as in Luke
9:31 and 24:25ff.? Was his interpretation singular or plural, and if the latter, was it in any way traditional? Such
questions are admissible but not wholly proper. He was
not so much resisting as transcending. If he was spiritual-
izing the exodus, it was a very earthy form of spiritualiz-
ing. His real concern was life and not death. Because Jesus
inaugurates a new kingdom of justice and freedom in his

death and resurrection, all previous understandings of kingdom, justice, and freedom are weighed, judged, and possibly redeemed. This process is conveyed by means of a dialogue with past views of kingdom, justice, and freedom, including the Exodus contributions to these concepts. The dialogue involves the following three points.

1. All is changed, but almost all is presented in a transformed mode. He does feed the poor, he does claim all power, his kingdom does include what is envisaged in the Magnificat. His hermeneutic is almost identical with that of Isaiah 43:14ff.; that is, the validity of the original model is affirmed, but it is understood in a new and living way that is controlled by the new thing and not by past interpretations. Almost all of the original revelatory event is usable once it is passed through the prism of the new event.

2. Christ interprets canonically. In Luke 24 the old "liberation" interpretation is countered by the whole canon of the law and prophets. The quotation from Isaiah 61 in Luke 4:18 is expounded by reference to 1 Kings 17 and 2 Kings 5:1–14.

3. As Childs has reminded us, the starting point for New Testament writers is the second Exodus rather than the first. Perhaps this tendency can be traced back to Jesus himself. By quoting from Isaiah 61 in his Nazareth sermon (Luke 4), Jesus himself seems to support this suggestion.

I have suggested that we use the Exodus theme as a way of understanding the canonical unity of the Bible. But I conclude with further questions. If you take a developing theme, how do you interpret it in your decision making? Do you take that theme at one juncture, and then, operating on the meaning found at that juncture, consciously begin listening for the echoes of the theme throughout scripture? Or do you start with the New Testament understanding of the Exodus? Does the fact that Christ seems to be hearing the Exodus message differently from the way it was commonly heard, certainly in Taiwan and in many similar situations, rule out earlier understandings of the Exodus?

The above discussion indicates some of the complexities involved when mission issues are brought to the canon. It is a personal discussion and a continuing one that gets no easier and seems endless, but as it proceeds, the conviction deepens that such discussions cannot be avoided. There is no easy road for today's mission if we follow our Lord. His missionary way is a narrow way and a hard way that demands the whole canon.

4

From Moses and All the Prophets:
A Canonical Approach to Interfaith Dialog

Introduction

In recent years we have witnessed a veritable flood tide of books, pamphlets, and articles treating religious pluralism, the Christian faith and other faiths, and dialogue among adherents of various faith traditions.

Lacking in all this outpouring is any sustained attempt to approach these important themes in a biblically comprehensive way. Citations from the Bible function merely to gloss a writer's point. An exception to this generalization is Wesley Ariarajah's *The Bible and People of Other Faiths* (1985). This work seeks to present a biblical apologetic for dialogue. Ariarajah takes up only a few select themes and treats them from the viewpoint of a pluralist-inclusivist theology of the religions.

The reasons for the paucity of satisfying treatments are legion. One is that "interfaith dialogue" is merely suffering, along with almost all other issues, from our inability to handle the Bible when it comes to making decisions either theological or ethical. In other words, it is one patient in a hospital of thousands who are awaiting treatment. Knowing better than ever what the Bible meant, we know little, and that with temerity, guilt, and hesitation, of what it means.

Some are not sure that a Bible completed almost two thousand years ago can speak about religions such as Buddhism and Hinduism, of which the biblical writers had no knowledge. And even if there is much about other faiths in the Bible, is there anything that we would recognize as "dialogue"? Dialogue with God, dialogue with the soul? Perhaps, but little that can be termed "interfaith dialogue." Is what we find in Acts 10–11, Mark 7:24ff., Acts 17, or John 4 recognizable as dialogue?

Does our use of the term "dialogue" allow it to include a conversation that within a very few minutes has one party saying, "Woman, you worship what you do not know; we worship what we know, for salvation is from the Jews," or, "Let the children first be fed, for it is not right to take the children's bread and throw it to the dogs"? These are but a few of the difficulties, yet sufficient to indicate, if such indication is necessary, the immensity of the problem.

The following treatment might be termed "postcredal" in the sense that it assumes that a Christian confession has been made and that this confession, although not pretending to have answered basic questions concerning the Bible, has adopted a "faith" stance toward it. This is not an avoidance of issues or blind obscurantism; it is following an epistemological road appropriate to the subject matter. Just as one uses a fork for certain foods and a spoon for others, so we know differently according to what we are knowing. We know God's word finally by faith and resist all attempts to say that it should be otherwise; and we are sorry for, and angry at, those who are spiritually undernourished because they insist that knowledge can come to us only on the forks of positivism and its progeny. The prongs that work admirably with some food are pitifully inadequate with the water of life.

A postcredal approach recognizes that there are questions about the unity, inspiration, authority, and canon of scripture. It also recognizes that there always have been questions and always will be in this life and that to await solution of even the greatest issues is to condemn oneself and the church not to inactivity but to activity that is most likely based on hidden creeds that come into operation when we fail to take our own seriously. And so we proceed, fully aware that we have said "credo" for epistemological as well as for pragmatic reasons, but also that we might understand in other ways what is implied in the unity, inspiration, authority, and canon of the Bible. To study these we must see them as operation-inspiring as well as being inspired, authorizing as well as being authoritative. To examine them in abstraction is to examine an unreality, and so a confessional acceptance of the Bible as scripture with all that implies is not a cutting of the Gordian knot because of impatience, or ignorance, or opposition to academe; it is, paradoxically, the way ultimately to untie it.

Before proceeding to the main argument, it is necessary to explain the first part of the title given to this chapter. "From Moses and All the Prophets" will be recognized as coming from the description of the risen Christ's preaching to his two disciples on the way to Emmaus (Luke 24). They had revealed their doubts and disillusion along with their impoverished understanding and their contentment with a "liberation theology": "But we had hoped that he was the one to redeem Israel" (v. 21). That Christ was sympathetic to their plight is revealed in his gentle approach in the guise of a stranger, but this does not prevent the rebuke: "O foolish men, and slow of heart to believe all that the prophets have spoken! Was it not necessary that the Christ should suffer these things and enter into his glory?" (v. 25–26). This was followed by an exposition from "all the scriptures" (v. 27), beginning with Moses and all the prophets—in other words, from the canon in its entirety as it was known in the first century before the writings were canonized.

The point of this "canonical" exposition was surely that nothing less than the canon as it existed was a sufficiently wide context in which to examine the prophecies of Christ's suffering and glory. The prophesying texts (the *testimonia*) were not sufficient, because in the case of the two disciples— as no doubt in the case of many others—these led only to a belief such as is outlined in Luke 24:19ff. Individual texts, as opposed to "Moses and all the prophets," had pointed to "a prophet mighty in deed and word" (v. 19), a Zealot liberator; they had not prepared men and women for Christ's death and resurrection. The preparation for these lay in the whole history of God's dealings with the people of God. Nearly two thousand years of election, covenant, bondage, exile, suffering, and contumely were necessary—a "dry bones" history, but one that culminated in a vision of a resurrected Israel. Only these could bear the weight of anticipating what would happen to the Son.

A canonical approach to an issue such as interfaith dialogue is unpopular to most and risible to some. This does not necessarily mean it is wrong. The alternatives are non-biblical studies or biblical studies that, lacking the self-correcting effect of the canon, are partial in both senses of the word. Fully aware of the pitfalls, I give, in outline, one attempt that I hope represents the internal dialogue within the Bible. I offer it as a contribution to further dialogue both inside the churches and between churches and other faiths.

The Argument

Of the kind of dialogue we are concerned with, the Bible shows little knowledge outside the Book of Job. In its pages are conversation, teaching, narrative, proclamation, witness, controversy, and more; there is perhaps what might be called "trialogue" because of the mediatorial nature of biblical faith. But on the whole, the fixed orders of society, with their clear roles and predetermined lines of authority, leave little room for something that presumes, among other things, a measure of equality. Even less, as noticed above, can we discern clear examples of what we would recognize as interfaith dialogue. Is then the venture doomed from the start, or are there ways of relating this alien question to the terminology and perhaps the "categories" of biblical thought? Is there a semantic and conceptual shift whereby we can transfer our problematic cargo to the biblical vessel? If there is little about dialogue, is there at least material about other faiths and their relation to Israel and the church that will give us a basis for our own understanding of dialogue?

Here great care is necessary. An immediate and easy answer to the question would be to begin with the plentiful material relating to idolatry, but this would be to fall into the error of choosing too narrow a context. Not to pay serious attention to the very important place assigned to the struggle against idols would be another form of partiality, one that is popular today; but to begin with idols would be disastrously prejudicial. A wider and less pejorative starting point must be sought, and such, I suggest, is present in the ubiquitous concern with the nations.

A serious view of the canon, with regard not only to its content but also to its ordering, reveals that the nations, their nature and prospect, not only are present from the primal history in Genesis 1–11 to Revelation but also are at the center of the Bible's concern. Before Abraham was, they are; and to them Abraham comes with the promise of blessing. If we accept that Genesis 1–11 is setting the stage for the drama of redemption, then it is difficult to avoid the conclusion that the appearance of the nations is the climax to which these eleven chapters are moving. They are the object of God's concern. The work of creation moves toward them, and the work of redemption, commencing with Abraham, begins with them and exists because of them.

Creation and redemption meet in the nations and in some sense revolve round them. And how are the nations presented? To this, chapters 10 and 11 respond, with little ambiguity, that the nations are wholly ambiguous. They are, according to Genesis 10, the work of God's hands, the result of God's blessing, and are "perfect" and pleasing, as is shown by their number—seventy, a theological rather than an arithmetical number. Their variety is viewed positively and almost celebrated. In contrast, chapter 11 sees them cursed by variety, separation, and alienation, knowing God only as judge. The setting for redemption, then, is creation and the nations, both of them both pleasing to God and displeasing, both blessed and cursed. They are the setting for redemption, not only chronologically in that they precede the call of Abraham but also because they—particularly the nations—are present theologically in every scene of the unfolding drama of redemption right up to the new heavens and the new earth, and the tree whose leaves are for the healing of the nations. To this matter of the omnipresent nations we will return later.

It may be asked—indeed, it should be asked—whether concentration on the nations is suitable when our question is about interfaith dialogue. Do the various nations represent the various faiths that Israel and the church encountered? Faiths and nations may not coincide in every instance; the overlap is not without exception, as in the case of the mystery religions of New Testament times that coincide with no specific nation. This must be admitted; nevertheless, the approach through the nations seems to be the best for two reasons:

1. The nations were, in the main, seen as corporate personalities in which people, monarch, and gods were bound together in one whole. A nation was its gods, its myths, and rituals rather than its politics, constitutions, and economics.

2. Because of the point noted above, we see in a nation a faith writ large; we see it in its most complete expression and not in some priestly or academic abstraction. We are able to see belief in its fullest context, which includes, as well as cult, the social institutions, laws, battles, buildings, and so forth, that makes more clear the inner faith.

This is step one in the argument—to enter the Bible via the court of the Gentiles. There are further steps, and the next and most crucial one is to recognize an even wider context in which the nations are set. As we will see later, the names for this context are numerous, far too numerous for clear and acceptable designation at this stage. Therefore, we will proceed slowly.

We have already noted that the Bible begins with creation and the nations, the latter being the climax and preparation for the election of a covenant with Abraham. The nations, therefore, belong to the pre-election period in the Bible, but not to the pre-covenant or pre-blessing period, as there are blessings abounding, on animals and people, before the promise of special blessing to Abraham, and as there is a specified covenant with Noah and creation and a presumed one with Adam also, long before Abraham.

We discover, then, early in the Bible, that the nations are associated with blessings—and curses—and with covenants before the blessing on Abraham and the covenant with him. The nations are there—varied, numerous, and established in Genesis 10; varied, numerous, and insecure in chapter 11—all before the call and commissioning of a chosen people. A distinction is beginning to appear. The nations are blessed, but not as Abraham is blessed, for his blessing will reach them only in the future. The nations are within a covenant, but not within the covenant with Abraham. And finally the nations are not elected. Israel, as Von Rad has pointed out, is deliberately omitted from the list of nations in chapter 10. Is this distinction between the nations and the chosen people, apparent in the early chapters of Genesis, maintained throughout the two Testaments? Essential to the argument proposed is that, despite a never-ending, ever-varying process of interaction and interdependence, the distinction is always there. As the thumb is to the fingers—serving by confronting; as male is to female—different, but together the image of God;

so the Bible presents the chosen people and the nations, always distinct but never separated.

If this is accepted, then our attempt to link the modern form of a problem, namely "interfaith dialogue," has led us near to the very center of the Bible's proclamation. A dialogue between the chosen and the nations lies at the heart of the economy of salvation. It is not something peripheral, a modern quirk, a trend, something forced upon us by easy communications and increasing emigration and immigration. Rather, it is of the essence of God's purpose; and if we would submit to that purpose, we must regard this dialogue with the utmost seriousness. No more serious regard can be paid than to see that our understanding of the dialogue conforms to that of the Bible. This is what we propose to do, and this is how we will order the doing of it.

First, we will examine the polarity that exists between creation and redemption or, alternatively, between creation and new creation. This will involve an emphasis on the distinction between two modes of God's activity in his world: God's work and God's "alien work," God's presence in creation and in redemption. Having stressed the distinction, we will then examine the inseparability of those factors that we have distinguished. Against this background of polarity or dialectic in which distinction and inseparability have been equally defended, we will examine the relationships between the chosen people (Israel/the church) and the nations. An understanding of these relationships, it is claimed, should provide guidelines, perhaps norms, for interfaith dialogue today, if we are prepared to admit continuity on the one hand between Israel/the church and the church of today and on the other hand between the Gentile faiths of the Bible and the faiths of today.

A concluding section will argue for a positive approach to dialogue, informed by the preceding analysis, on the grounds that dialogue rightly understood is essential to God's purpose and, therefore, to the church's identity and mission.

The Divine Dialectic: Creation and Redemption

T. E. Hulme says in *Speculations:*

> One of the main achievements of the nineteenth
> century was the elaboration and universal applica-
> tion of the principle of continuity. The destruction of
> this conception is, on the contrary, an urgent neces-
> sity of the present.... This shrinking from a gap or
> jump in nature has developed to a degree which
> paralyses any objective perception, and prejudices
> our seeing things as they really are. For an objective
> view of reality we must make use both of categories
> of continuity and discontinuity. Our principal con-
> cern then, at the present moment, should be the re-
> establishment of the temper or disposition of mind
> which can look at a gap or chasm without shudder-
> ing (1924:3–4).

Hulme was not speaking primarily of theology, and therefore *mutatis mutandis* must preface any application of his
words to our concern. Nevertheless the links are there. Has
not the mood that produced Hulme's "shrinking from a gap"
been at least partially responsible for so much theological
shrinking from distinctions: the distinctions between God
and humankind, supernatural and natural, transcendent and
immanent, and the consequent tendency for theology to be
absorbed into anthropology; the distinction between heaven
and earth and their dissolution into the universe; the distinction between right and wrong in a world of moral rela-
tivism; perhaps even the distinction between male and
female in an increasing unisexual culture?

The shuddering at gaps or chasms has had its theological and religious counterparts for a very long time, and the
means for avoiding the shudders are numerous. Israel
wanted at times to absorb Yahwism into a modified
Baalism; much Christian heresy has centered around

attempts to deny the distinction of the two natures in Christ and the three persons in the Trinity. We move naturally to a monism or an ontocracy and retreat from distinction at the heart of things as unnatural and threatening. The previous paragraph has indicated certain modern features of this perpetual avoidance of the shudder, but one remains as yet unmentioned. Up to and beyond the Reformation, the redemptive work of God in Christ was given the central position in Christian faith and practice, but with due recognition of God's work as creator and sustainer of all things. Although this distinction between God's work as creator and his work as redeemer was against the human tendency to deny the distinctiveness that we have spoken about, the acceptance of scriptural authority and the scriptures' plain witness to the two activities preserved creation and redemption in a somewhat tense and uneasy balance. The missionary movement of the nineteenth century tended to stress the doctrine of redemption to the neglect of God's work and presence in creation. The laudable, faithful, sacrificial proclamation of Christ to the heathen world was done with the biblical emphasis that the world's salvation depended upon it, but at the same time was forgetful of the equally biblical emphasis that "the earth is the Lord's and the fullness thereof." "Deepest and darkest Africa" was deep and dark not only because the gospel of Christ had not been preached there, or because Africans were "separated from Christ, alienated from the commonwealth of Israel and strangers to the covenants of promise, having no hope and without God in the world," (Eph. 2:12) but also because God's "other presence," in every leaf and thought and breath, was largely overlooked.

How far the forgetfulness of God's omnipresence was due to changing views of scripture and the advances of natural science, or how far it contributed to the imperialism practiced by the West—or did the imperialism contribute to the forgetfulness?—these belong to other studies. Our present interest is confined to pointing out a denial or at least a modifying of a distinction. The dialectic in God's working was muted by suppressing one side.

Soon after the turn of the century, the reaction began to appear (Amos 9:7 reared its de-contextualized head early) and already by the end of the Second World War had shown signs of becoming dominant. The shudder was not avoided by stressing creation at the expense of redemption. God was present everywhere. Had God not created all things and seen that they were very good? Had God not been present with Assyria (Isaiah 10) and with Babylon (cf. Jeremiah)? Had not Deutero-Isaiah referred to Cyrus as Messiah? Emphases on John 1:9, Acts 17, Malachi 1:11, and others, soon followed. Inevitably, the need for taking God to where God was already present was questioned. Mission ceased to be proclamation of Good News and became "discerning where God was at work and cooperating with him." Creation apparently included redemption; all were saved, but especially the poor and oppressed, even though some received salvation anonymously—a kind of *aegrotat* degree received *in absentia* by a nonmatriculant who opposed tertiary education. The flight from biblical distinction into philosophical fantasy has continued until there is almost a received "orthodoxy" where "creation" is so dominant and "new creation" so suppressed that mission is seen as springing from contempt, not love, and where it is heretical to question the dogma that all prayers, no matter how addressed, are directed to and received by God. All that remains is the ultimate step of proclaiming *in ecclesia nulla salus*.

Before examining the forms of distinction in the Bible, let me ask, with temerity, wherein lies the origin of the distinctions? Is it sin? Is it rooted in the division between heaven and earth, or in the separation between God the creator and the created heaven and earth? Is it possible to find a more original origin than these? Does not a passage like Hosea 11 suggest that it is? Does the source of dialectic not lie in God's own nature? If we can penetrate beneath the layers of Christian theology, compounded with philosophies alien to the Bible, is there not apparent a "dialogue" in the heart of God? In Hosea 11:1–4, the love of God struggles with Israel's sin; in verses 5–7, God's anger triumphs: "The sword shall rage against their cities... so they are appointed to the yoke, and none shall remove it" (11:6–7). But then come verses 8–9: "How can I give you up, O Ephraim! How can I hand you over, O Israel!... My heart recoils within me, my compassion grows warm and tender. I will not execute my fierce anger, I will not again destroy Ephraim; for I am God and not man, the Holy One in your midst, and I will not come to destroy." Primitive? Anthropomorphic? But it is precisely anthropomorphism that is being denied: "I am God and not man." Can we not say here there is a glimpse of that distinctiveness necessary to dialectic and to dialogue which later is seen more clearly in Paul's "the goodness and the severity of God," in the cry of dereliction on the cross, and in the work of the Father and the work of the Son?

Distinction

Because this is an outline, brevity is demanded. But brevity will also suffice, for what is being argued lies on the surface of the Old and New Testaments and most of the great theologies, namely, that God offers himself redeemingly to a world that God claims and where he works unceasingly, neither slumbering nor sleeping. God in Christ has come to his own; in the church God's nature and word are proclaimed to a creation and to nations that are the work of his hand and are sustained by the word of his power.

This duality is abundantly recognized in the history of Christian thought. Expressions such as natural theology and revealed theology, general revelation and special revelation have been common currency for most of the church's history. John Calvin's *Institutes* begin with a book on "The Knowledge of God the Creator" and continue with Book II on "The Knowledge of God the Redeemer." In Book I, chapter II.1 he writes: "First, in the fashioning of the universe and in the general teaching of scripture the Lord shows himself to be the Creator. Then in the face of Christ (cf. 2 Cor. 4:6) he shows himself to be the Redeemer. Of the resulting two-fold knowledge of God we shall now discuss the first aspect; the second will be dealt with in its proper place." Karl Barth's *Church Dogmatics* devotes Volume III to the doctrine of creation and Volume IV to the doctrine of reconciliation, and in two famous sections entitled "Creation as the External Basis of the Covenant" and "The Covenant as the Internal Basis of Creation," he distinguishes the twofold work of God while at the same time showing their interdependence.

Much theological writing since early in the nineteenth century has centered on the term "salvation history" (*Heilsgeschichte*) and related terms; for example, "antihistory" and "history created by the word of God." This is in contrast to "history," although the two are never separable. In *Salvation in History* Oscar Cullmann writes:

> A positive relationship to history in general is established by the fact that salvation history involves a sequence of events taking place within history. Salvation history is, therefore, not a history alongside history, it unfolds in history, and in this sense belongs to it. As soon as we examine this sequence more closely, fundamental distinctions arise, proving that despite this contact, salvation history and history can in no case be equated (1967:153).

The fact of the distinction between creation and redemption in theological thought is so manifest that it needs no further mention, and the only reason for referring to it at all is because it is assumed that it reflects a similar distinction in the Bible itself. I assume that such a distinction is present in many and various forms throughout the Bible. Only a sample of the terms used and little mention of the usage will suffice to indicate what will be already known to the reader. It is recognized that the variety of terms and categories will introduce some whose significance is not identical with the terms "creation" and "redemption." However, I will introduce only those terms and categories that have sufficient overlap with "creation" and "redemption" to reinforce the contention that God has a twofold presence and a dual work in the world and that the nations with their faith belong with the creation presence, whereas Israel and the church belong with the nations and are yet representative of the second and redemptive presence.

Blessings

In Genesis 1:22, 28, God blesses the living creatures and humankind, and in the strength of this blessing bids them multiply and be fruitful. This blessing is part of the creative process and is given indiscriminately to the designated categories. It requires no response but that of usage, and is impersonal. A similar blessing appears in Genesis 9:1. Again it is given to humankind and requires no response other than usage.

In Genesis 12:1ff., a blessing comes to Abraham that requires the response of obedience. It belongs to a chosen part of humankind and needs to be transferred personally (cf. Israel's blessing of Jacob). The nations will find it in the future only via Abraham's descendants (Gen. 12:3). Blessings, therefore, come in two distinct ways: in association with creation and in association with a chosen people whose presence and work are to represent God's redemption.

Covenants

With Genesis 9:8 God establishes a covenant with Noah and his descendants and with every living creature. It is also a covenant that restricts the flood water, preserves the earth, and is witnessed to by the rainbow in the heavens. It is a "creation" covenant replacing a presumed one with Adam. Such covenants are found elsewhere in the Old Testament; for example, Jeremiah 33:25 and Hosea 2:18. Like "creation" blessings, they are impersonal, unconditioned, indiscriminate; they establish the natural order and are the conditions of human life; they require no response.

Along with the new blessing, the advent of a chosen people introduces a second order of covenant (Gen. 17:4), the forerunner of a considerable variety. Some are conditional; for example, Exodus 19–24 and Joshua 24. Some are unconditional—supremely the covenant with David. But all of them, including the new covenant in Christ's blood, are limited, personal, requiring the response of obedience, and associated with those chosen by God to represent his redemptive work.

A People Among the Nations

In Numbers 23:9, Balaam reports, "For from the top of the mountains I see him, from the hills I behold him; lo, a people dwelling alone, and not reckoning itself among the nations!" Sometimes in the Old Testament Israel is referred to as a "nation," but usually the linguistic usage supports Balaam's contention that Israel did not reckon itself among the nations. The Hebrew distinction between 'am (people) and goiim (nations) continues into the Septuagint and the New Testament with the use of laos and ethnos, the church becoming the Israel of God and, like Israel, distinguished from the nations. As we have seen above, the nations appear as part of creation, whereas the people of Israel and their successors, the church, appear only with the second order of blessings and covenants, and are associated with them.

Other Terms

A book by John Reumann (1973) begins with "a certain tension between creation and redemption" in the Apostles' and Nicene creeds, and then proceeds to discuss the tension in the Bible in terms of "creation" and "new creation," drawing the latter term from Galatians 6:15 and 2 Corinthians 5:17.

A thorough investigation of the terms and images used to designate God's strange redemptive instrument of Israel/the church and to contrast it with the rest of creation would be intimidating; almost every page of the Bible would suggest new possibilities. Israel is the chosen, the called, the elected, the bride, the peculiar people, a holy people, a nation of priests, God's inheritance, the servant of Jahweh, and so forth. When we turn to the New Testament the list continues. Some of the old terms such as "bride" and "Israel" are applied to the church; some are new creations themselves. The church is contrasted with the world, the children of light with the children of darkness; the church is a temple, and the body of Christ. The imagery of a second birth alone provides considerable richness of expression, for those "born again," "born of water and the Spirit" are contrasted with those born of the flesh, the latter belonging to "creation," the second-born belonging to "redemption."

A point must not be overlabored or the argument becomes counterproductive. I have run the risk of overemphasizing the obvious, because there is much resistance to any consideration of the distinction. What are the reasons for opposing what to some is exceedingly plain and straightforward? This question has already been referred to above, but further consideration is necessary before proceeding.

Often answers are rejected not because they are untrue but because possible motives behind the answer arouse suspicion. It is feared that this is sometimes the case in the present issue. In the heat of religious and theological debate, the kind of distinction insisted upon above can be dismissed as "triumphalist," "conservative," "right wing," "Western imperialist," "interventionist," or even as "theological racism." Proponents of the distinction may be condemned as "white supremacists," "defenders of Christendom," and a host of other irrelevant names, all of which ignore the fact that even a "racist" is neither lying nor deceiving when he says 2 + 2 = 4, or that the most egalitarian lover of all humankind can, on occasion, talk nonsense. In other words, we are dealing with an emotive issue, and the emotion sometimes obscures what may not be welcome but is very clear.

Granting that our theology should be postcredal, and granting also that the Bible is in some sense normative and that there is a place for hearing what it says even if we disagree most heartily, are there still reasons why the above distinction is denied? I think there are.

First, the distinction is sometimes made without an equally strong emphasis being given to the inseparability, interpenetration, and interdependence of those elements that are nevertheless distinguishable. In other words, the discontinuity is sometimes not balanced with the complementary continuity. This I will attempt to do in what follows.

Second, the distinction is unwelcome to the present age—perhaps to every age—and, therefore, presuppositions and preunderstandings (combined with premisunderstandings) counter the self-evident before it has time to show its evidence.

Third, this chapter is not elucidating or fortifying. To do so would be to run the risk of going back on a determination to be postcredal; that is, to evaluate the reasonableness of a scriptural teaching on the basis of an external belief that is most likely to be at variance with Christian belief. The distinction at issue, no matter how unwelcome or unreasonable, if it is truly there, is part of our starting point; it belongs to the norm. It is the judge and not the judged, the measuring rod and not the line measured.

Fourth, a sophisticated age, so accustomed to complexity, is appalled by simplicity or what at one level appears uncomplicated.

Fifth, and partly in contrast with the previous point, insufficient thought is paid to the nature and complexity of relationships. The close connection between creation and redemption in such books as Deutero-Isaiah or in New Testament passages that speak of Christ as the agent and sustainer of creation (for example, John 1:3, 10; Col. 1:16; Heb. 1:2) leads some to oppose any real division between them! Determined to join creation and redemption, some minds refuse any distinction; in defense of a continuity they are blind to the obvious discontinuity. Relationships between inanimate objects can be varied in the extreme; relations between persons are so rich that each is *sui generis*. How much more intricate, subtle, and wonderful is the many-colored splendor of God's tapestry, with its warp of creation and woof of redemption! Or is it the warp of redemption and the woof of creation?

Inseparability

In the sections that lie ahead, I will deal at some length with the multiplicity of relationships between Israel/the church and the nations extending throughout the canon. This will show in detail the interdependence of what are two major factors in God's twofold working. But they are part and not the whole. The present section is designed briefly to speak of this interdependence and inseparability on the wider canvas of creation and redemption and their related covenants. A truth that is widely expressed and everywhere assumed—even in the Wisdom literature—can be referred to only by sample. I have attempted to chose significant ones.

I am assuming that the relationship between the old and new covenants is such as can best be understood if we use the model of a straight line. Jesus fulfills the promises of the Old Testament; the church continues the responsibility first committed to Israel. On the other hand, the relationship between the creation and redemption covenants is best visualized as concentric circles that are never wholly apart and that at times reveal their common center by showing similarities of form and function and mutual reflection.

Genesis 1:1–2:4a (the P account of creation) recounts the ordering of all creation. Beginning with a chaotic conglomeration that was "without form and void," God regulates and divides, making chaos give place to order. From the moment the Spirit "broods" over the chaotic waters of the "abyss" there is the hint of redemption in the air, for order is redemptive as well as creative, and where chaos is overcome salvation is reflected in the victory. Thus from the start creation is tinged with the light of its other pole.

The interrelatedness continues through the primal history. Human disobedience was followed by more than punishment. First, the punishment was less than could be expected: the sinning pair were not killed; they were reprieved. Second, the very punishment was gracious: to be expelled from the garden was punitive but was also a mark of God's loving consideration. Life in the garden might have resulted in eating of the tree of life and living forever: eternal life before the fall might have been possible, but eternal life for the unredeemed sinner would have meant increasing suffering. Expulsion, in preserving the pair from the "danger" of living forever, was therefore of grace. Third, God covered the shameful pair when their own concealment was insufficient, thereby showing his acceptance of them in their new role of sinner. Once more the redemption that had yet to come was casting its shadow before it. Cain's punishment, like his father's, was mixed with grace, and his brand was gracious and punitive because it protected him. After the flood, the remnant—redemption motif—was preserved in a stable, reliable environment; blessings and a rainbow were given them; vegetarian restrictions were removed and God repented! Only the Babel story is graceless, but this is for the good reason that it is deliberately so in order to preface the grace that follows in Abraham and the whole of remaining scripture.

Examples of the inseparability of creation and redemption covenants appear in Hosea and Jeremiah. In Hosea the redemption covenant between Yahweh and Israel is to the fore, particularly in conjunction with the marriage image. Israel has broken covenant by going after her "lovers," the baals. God will punish but will restore the broken covenant eventually. In chapter 2, the covenant between Israel and Yahweh is closely interwoven with the creation theme. Israel forsakes Yahweh because she thinks the baals control creation (Hos. 2:5). God declares that it is God who controls and not the baals (2:8), and God will demonstrate this by withdrawing the fruits of blessing (2:9, 12). However, this is not the end; there is a future for both covenants in which they are so interrelated that they are almost one. In Hosea 2:18 we read, "And I will make for you a covenant on that day with the beasts of the field, the birds of the air...; and I will abolish the bow, the sword, and war from the land; and I will make you lie down in safety." This is immediately followed by redemption covenant language in versus 19 and 20: "And I will betroth you to me for ever; I will betroth you to me in righteousness and in justice, in steadfast love, and in mercy. I will betroth you to me in faithfulness; and you shall know the LORD." This is immediately followed in verse 21 by a return to the language of creation covenant but with a highly unusual change. The covenant affirming God's control of nature and therefore providing assurance that God would meet Israel's material needs is a covenant that operates like a redemption covenant. It is not wholly automatic; rather, it functions by a process of prayer and response: "I will answer the heavens and they shall answer the earth; and the earth shall answer the grain, the wine, and the oil." Now both covenants require response. The redemption covenant is here not merely foreshadowed in a creation covenant, but is influencing its content and form.

The prophet Jeremiah prefaces his famous prophecy of the new covenant with words reminiscent of the creation passage in Hosea 2:23: "Behold, the days are coming, says the LORD, when I will sow the house of Israel and the house of Judah" (Jer. 31:27). Then, following after the new covenant prophecy, he returns to creation language in 31:35–36: "Thus says the LORD, who gives the sun for light by day and the fixed order of the moon and the stars for light by night...: 'If this fixed order departs from before me, says the LORD, then shall the descendants of Israel cease from being a nation before me for ever.'" Thus the redemption covenant is bracketed by creation covenant language, although the word "covenant" is not actually used in the brackets. Moreover, in addition to the bracketing effect, there is an even closer connection in Jeremiah 31:36–37, where, in two separate statements, the fixity and dependability of the creation covenant are given as a guarantee of the redemptive covenant.

In Jeremiah 33:19–26 the same kind of usage and argumentation appears, but with even greater clarity because the word "covenant" is used of both God's creation and redemption work: "Thus says the LORD: If you can break my covenant with the day and my covenant with the night, so that day and night will not come at their appointed time, then also my covenant with David my servant may be broken, so that he shall not have a son to reign on his throne, and my covenant with the Levitical priests my ministers" (Jer. 33:20–21; cf. also vv. 22, 25–26).

Creation and redemption themes are nowhere more closely intertwined than in Isaiah 40–55. The question of how they are related has received much attention in recent Old Testament writings. Von Rad argues that creation is (as always) never an independent doctrine but always subservient to the redemption theme, while Carroll Stuhlmueller uses the expression "creative redemption." By this he means that creation expresses God's redemptive work now. Creation is "a wondrous... act of Jahweh" now—a redemptive act "bringing to Israel a new national existence and a new prosperity of unprecedented scope with creative repercussions upon all the elements of Israel's existence, even upon the cosmos" (Reumann 1973:78). I have referred only fleetingly to the discussion, because the details of whether creation is subordinate to redemption or whether the relationship can be more correctly defined are not germane to the issue before us. Here we are concerned only with their very close connection and interdependence about which there can be no doubt: it is apparent almost everywhere in Deutero-Isaiah. But let us not forget to note that in spite of this, and in spite of there being a "mission" on the creation/history side, perhaps few writings in the Bible are so far removed from the spirit of much modern writing about dialogue and so insistent upon mission, witness, the word, and the place of Israel. Although Deutero-Isaiah has hammered out his gospel in Babylon and welcomes Cyrus of Persia, he approaches neither of these nations with "dialogue humility" and is more outspoken about the "no-gods" of the nations than any of his predecessors.

The New Testament, no less than the Old Testament, preserves the inseparability of creation and redemption as well as their distinction. The birth of the savior is welcomed by the appearance of a star; his death is marked by the withholding of light. He demonstrates his creative power by miracles such as the turning of water into wine and the feeding of the five thousand. His control of the sea is a significant theme that, against the mythical background of the rebellious waters, is a clear demonstration that the natural order is secure and stable because he is its sovereign.

In the historical realm, all things "conspire" to fulfill God's purpose of redemption. Caesar Augustus's census

ensures the Messiah's birth in Bethlehem, Pilate's character and Roman law his death in Jerusalem. The theological
implications of what the evangelists state are sometimes
found in the Gospels—for example, the prologue to John's
Gospel—but more often in the epistles: Romans 8:19,
Ephesians 1:10, 1 Corinthians 2:7, and supremely
Colossians 1:15–20 link Christ's creative and redemptive
tasks. He, who is the word and agent of creation, is the
agent of the new creation, and in Revelation the new heavens and the new earth, the new Jerusalem, and the healed
nations appear only because of the suffering, death, and
resurrection of the victorious Christ.

The concentric circles of creation/history and redemption belong always together, distinct as man and wife are
distinct, but joined by God and not to be put asunder.

The People and the Nations:
Interfaith Relations in the Bible

In what has preceded I have argued for a twofold working
of God in the world but with equal stress upon both the
inseparability of the two modes of working and their distinction. We now turn to two aspects of the biblical
record—the people of God, both Israel and the church, and
the nations—with the intention of examining their distinctiveness and inseparability. We do this with two convic-
tions: first, that the nations belong primarily to the work of
God we have referred to under the rubric "creation
covenant," and that the people of God, although belonging
also within this covenant, are, and more significantly, representative of the redemption covenant; second, it is
believed that an understanding of the "interfaith" relationships within the Bible will provide us with normative material for the better understanding of interfaith relations and,
in particular, interfaith dialogue in the present.

After a brief summary of the extent of Israel's associations
with the surrounding nations, we will attempt to analyze the

cardinal features of the relationships. Then we will consider the much briefer period covered by the New Testament writings and will ask whether Christ, the apostles, and the church, in their relationships with the Gentiles, experienced anything comparable to what is found in the Old Testament. In other words, is there a discernible pattern of relationships that is common to both the old and new covenants? If there is, then the argument for seeking a biblical norm would be considerably strengthened.

Israel and the Nations: The Extent of the Relationship

Israel's history is a history among the nations as well as a history before God, and most of the books of the Old Testament could be studied in a triangular fashion—Israel relating to God in the light of her relations with one or more of the nations.

We have already noted that in Genesis the nations appear long before the people of Israel. Israel has no direct, aboriginal, mythical relationship with God. In Genesis 10 Israel is not present except as a possibility hidden in the loins of the otherwise undistinguished Arpachshad. The nations are her matrix, and all that divides her from them is the call of God, spoken first to Abraham. This call comes to him as a member of one of the nations; according to the dominant tradition it was the nation that included "Ur of the Chaldees." Abraham, however, is not permitted to have an unambiguous origin, for another tradition locates his home in Haran. What is not in doubt (but cf. Ezek. 16:3), though, is the Semitic origins that mean an early connection with the Arabian peninsula and its nomads.

Abraham, called so emphatically to forsake his roots (Gen. 12:1), with the utmost difficulty and threatened in every way, even by God, eventually begins to establish his clan. But this he does as a rootless man on alien ground in constant interaction with peoples of a variety of nations, cultures, and faiths: Canaanites, Egyptians, Hittites, and so forth. Most significant are his relationships with the residents of Canaan and Egypt; the outline of that very intricate link with Egypt, constantly being elaborated and developed even into the New Testament, was already appearing. Isaac, but much more Jacob, continues the contacts until the chosen ones become resident and almost lost in Egypt, having got there through Egyptian generosity, Midianite slave trading, and possibly Hyksos hegemony.

Israel's "second birth" was not among Semites—if Ur was indeed truly Semitic in Abraham's time—but among the Egyptians with the help of the Kenites, that most ambiguous of nations, descendants of that most ambiguous of men—the man Cain. The exodus from Egypt is followed by forty years of "education," in constant relationship with the inhabitants of nations surrounding the promised land. Warfare in some countries and negotiations with others bring the Israelites to Moab and eventually to more warfare and the gradual subjugation of the many peoples domiciled in Canaan. The time of the judges was a time when Israel was never allowed to forget the foreign enemy, and the word of God was heard, forgotten, and remembered in the ceaseless confrontation with the threats and temptations that came to them from their unneighborly neighbors. The human link between the time of the judges and the monarchy was the Philistines. Their system of government, more centralized than that of Israel and therefore more efficient, was at once the menace and the entry of the fissionable tribes. After some hesitation, divine permission through Samuel sanctioned the establishment of the monarchy, and a new era including greatly expanded international relations began.

The Books of Samuel, Kings, and the later prophets might be characterized as accounts of kings, God and nation, and prophets, God and nations. The time of Saul was lived in the shadow of the Philistines, and the same shadow extended well into David's reign. David, after being a Philistine mercenary, not only related to the Gentiles but also subjugated sufficient numbers of them to establish his own empire and employ his own mercenaries. Solomon, relating through a marriage treaty even to Egypt, relates too well. His "dialogue" with other faiths, like that of the later Ahab, was far too humble and sympathetic, and his own faith was corrupted. Omri organized many of the nations into a defensive bloc; Elijah and Elisha prophesied when the Syrians were in the ascendant; Amos and Hosea combated Canaanite influence and along with Isaiah spoke to the accompaniment of Assyrian jackboots. Take Babylon from the Books of Jeremiah and Ezekiel and Babylon and Persia from Deutero-Isaiah, and the remaining picture is frameless. And let it not be forgotten that as the kings married with the nations, studied the nations, borrowed, lent, and traded with the nations, fought with the nations, overcame and succumbed to the nations, the prophets threatened, warned, and cursed the nations, only occasionally promising them a future, but a future that centered on Zion. Jeremiah, to whom was committed the foreknowledge of the new covenant, was actually appointed as "prophet to the nations."

The tale is long and further elaboration perhaps pointless, because the point is obvious even from a great distance— almost any book in the Old Testament is trialogical: it is a trialogue that includes Israel, the nations, and God, and in which Israel hears God's word in her strange wrestle with the nations. As Jacob sees the face of God in the face of his ghostly but powerful adversary (Genesis 32), so his descendants see God's face as they are locked in blessed confrontation with the nations.

Israel and the Nations: The Relationship Analyzed

An examination of Israel's connections with the nations has resulted in the elucidation of four major categories and several minor subcategories. The major ones are as follows: (1) Israel existed for the nations; (2) Israel's life was lived over against the nations; (3) Israel lived a debtor to the nations; (4) Israel was called to be a missionary to the nations.

The analysis is tentative and done with full awareness (a) that the categories are not as clearcut as they might appear to be and (b) that any attempt to analyze and dissect what comes largely in images, stories, visions, poems, praises, and auditions can be fatal to the truth and to the confidence of the analyst. What follows is little more than a summary of conclusions; the dissecting room is large, disordered, and bloody.

Israel Existed (Exists?) for the Nations

The juxtaposition of Abraham's call and the primal history has already been referred to above and its significance suggested. In this I am following a long tradition that has received strong support in much modern exegesis, in theological writing, and in missiology. Israel is presented as the grace absent from the graceless tower of Babel story. In the sudden narrowing of focus from the widest possible, namely, creation and the nations, down to one man and his successors, in whom the nations would bless themselves, are we not meant to see Israel's *raison d'être* as an existence for the nations? Israel was called to be a nation of priests, a holy people, a servant of Jahweh to the nations, a light to the nations, the custodian of Zion to which the nations should come. "Missionary" texts can be found in the Old Testament, and I will refer to some of them later, but they are not very numerous because the time for true mission had not yet come, and Israel's calling was first and foremost to exist for the nations, to be a presence—to live before God and before the nations. Perhaps this is the meaning of the strange expression in Genesis 12:3 that sees the blessed Abraham not so much as blessing as being the one in whom the nations should bless themselves.

Israel's Life Was Lived Over Against the Nations

When the subject of Israel's relations with other cultures, countries, and faiths is raised, we instinctively think of relationships of conflict and controversy: the warnings against idolatry and apostasy; the tales of persecution, warfare, bloodshed, and heroism in the face of the enemy; the slaughter of worshipers of other gods; David killing the Philistine Goliath; Samuel hewing Agag in pieces; Psalm 137; Moses bringing the plagues on Pharaoh. These are what first spring to mind, and without doubt this is the majority opinion of the Old Testament writers. We will distinguish four somewhat different manifestations of the conflict.

1. *The nations as enemies.* Humanly speaking, there were good reasons why neighboring nations should frequently be seen as enemies. On the journey to the promised land, Israel was invading the territory of other people even if her intention was not to conquer. On reaching the promised land, the inhabitants were naturally inimical to what, to them, was unprovoked aggression, conquest, and oppression. Having established themselves at the crossroads of the world, it was little wonder that the sound of tramping armies was rarely a distant one, and usually, and understandably, the armies wanted to exchange Israel's control of the territory for their own. Finally, Israel's uncertain possession of the land was disputed for the last time, and, beginning with the Assyrians, a series of conquerors was seen as the perpetual enemy, because they ruled over God's gift to God's people.

Apart from a brief period, during the reigns of David and Solomon when a combination of Israel's strength and certain external factors made for a kind of peace, the enemy was either within the gate or not far from it.

2. *The nations as God's instrument of punishment.* In the previous section I was "humanly speaking," looking at

the human causes for military threat. But sometimes, and no doubt more often than the Bible makes explicit, the foreign menace had superhuman as well as human causation. Beginning at least in the time of the judges, God showed control of all nations and deep displeasure with Israel by using the nations as a means of punishing the people of God. The Canaanites, the Midianites, the Philistines, Assyria, and Babylon are some of the nations so used, and explicit references are found in Judges and many of the prophets, the best known being Isaiah 10.

3. *The nations as witness to Israel's rebellion.* Amos 3:11 speaks of an adversary surrounding the land of Israel. This is in accord with the preceding paragraph. But in Amos 3:9 we find a motif that is not unique but is less common—nations are asked to come and bear witness: "Proclaim to the strongholds in Assyria, and to the strongholds in the land of Egypt, and say, 'Assemble yourselves upon the mountains of Samaria, and see the great tumults within her, and the oppressions in her midst.'"

4. *The nations as a religious threat to Israel.* This is a major theme in the Old Testament and might be said to be the text on which the sermon of Deuteronomy is preached. Set in the midst of the nations, to live in behalf of the nations, Israel runs the constant risk of being seduced by them into idolatry, polytheism, apostasy. Deuteronomy 7:1–5 makes the danger explicit. Deuteronomy 13 is a measure of its seriousness; the Books of Kings turn on the question of whether the kings succumbed to the threat or resisted it; and the prophets tirelessly oppose such feckless "adultery" with the gods of the nations.

Israel as a Debtor to the Nations

Our knowledge of Israel's indebtedness is in large part based upon the biblical literature itself, but some comes from the result of modern discovery. In five subsections we will merely hint at the vast deposits of material at our disposal.

1. *Egypt.* Israel's relationship with Egypt is so special that it must be looked at separately. Undoubtedly, Egypt is the enemy par excellence; she is Rahab, the embodiment of evil, the oppressor. But this is not all; she plays another role. Beginning with Abraham, the chosen people turn to Egypt in their extremity. Jacob is well treated there; Joseph rises to a place of great power; Moses is indebted to Egypt for education and his "culture." He is regarded by his future relations as an Egyptian, and he is indeed a "prince" in Egypt.

The Exodus is an escape from the prison of Egypt, but in "coming out" of Egypt is there not the suggestion that Egypt was the womb that gave Israel birth, as Ur of the Chaldees gave birth to Abraham? Is not Egypt both protector and matrix of Israel as well as bondmaster and oppressor? And the ambiguous relationship continues: David and Solomon turn to Egypt for guidance in administrative matters, and Solomon finds a wife there; Ahijah the prophet of the schism looks to Egypt; Jeremiah flees to Egypt. So great is the debt to this one country that the history of Israel with Egypt subtracted is totally unimaginable, and the debt is by no means only for centuries of educative suffering.

2. *Cultural borrowing.* Archaeology and changed patterns of theological thought have enabled us to acknowledge how much Israel took from surrounding cultures. The language we know as "Hebrew" was, as Isaiah informs us, "the lip of Canaan." Many of Israel's laws show so much affinity with those of other nations that they must share a common origin. Israel's three main festivals are generally recognized to be transformed borrowings, comparable to our own Christmas and Easter. Fragments of wisdom and covenant formulations—these are but a few of the signs of Israel's indebtedness. This continuity with other cultures is balanced by a corresponding discontinuity, for as the people of Israel matched their borrowing skills with an even

greater skill in transforming what was borrowed. The new patch was preshrunk so that it strengthened and adorned the old without tearing it.

3. *The nations as occasion for revelation.* The bondage in Egypt was the occasion for the greatest demonstration of God's redemptive power, and this set a pattern. The monarchy that, after David, is certainly seen as revelatory comes to Israel because of pressure from the Philistines. The prophets make their greatest pronouncements of God's words at those junctions of Israel's history when relations with the nations have grown critical. It might almost be said that without the interference of a nation or nations Israel rarely hears the word of the Lord.

4. *The nations as instruments of liberation.* The supreme example of this theme is found in the prophecies of Deutero-Isaiah. The exiles in Babylon had long endured their second "bondage." Now the second "Exodus" was at hand, an "Exodus" that stretched out into eschatological time but which began with the conquests of Cyrus the Persian. So great was this hope of liberation—a hope that was wholly justified—that Cyrus is given the title of "messiah" (Isa. 45:1).

5. *The good pagans.* In contrast to most of the Old Testament, some writers take pleasure—almost a perverse pleasure—in pointing to the excellent in the nations as though Israel should be made aware of her debt to them for good examples. Esau, who was later regarded as symbolic of the Gentiles, is shown to be more of the gentleman than his chosen brother Jacob. Pharaoh shows up much better than the timid liar Abraham, who is prepared to sacrifice Sarah to save his own skin. The sailors in the Book of Jonah are splendid fellows, and the people of Nineveh the most ready converts imaginable, once given a chance to believe. If we take note of Rahab, we see that even the harlots in Canaan are helpful and dependable, and when Israel wants to describe an ideal woman she turns to the

Moabitess Ruth. In her better moments, Israel did not allow her sense of election to obscure the virtues in others, virtues that put her in the nations' debt.

Israel as Missionary to the Nations

This point has been documented by H. H. Rowley, Robert Martin-Achard, Johannes Blauw, and others. In some ways it is an extension of the first category—Israel existing for the nations. But it deserves separate mention because at times Israel is more than a presence: she is more active; she is called to mission.

1. *Centripetal mission.* Mission in the New Testament begins at Jerusalem and spreads outward: "Go ye into all the world..." In the Old Testament it can be said that mission is often seen to end at Jerusalem. Particularly in the prophets (for example, Isa. 2:2ff.) there is a vision of the nations coming to Jerusalem where they will find the Torah and the Word. This has been termed "centripetal mission," although it must be noted that this can be combined with "centrifugal mission"—"For out of Zion shall go forth the law, and the word of the LORD from Jerusalem" (Isa. 2:3). That centripetal mission is also present in the New Testament.

2. *Other ways of doing mission.* Israel's existence, its identity, was founded not so much on race, geography, and culture as on covenant: an Israelite was someone who made and kept covenant with Jahweh. Thus from the beginning the "stranger" could technically cease to be a stranger and become one of the "children." Incorporation into Israel was always potentially possible, and therefore the covenant was an instrument of mission.

Some passages have been widely referred to as "missionary passages." Best known are the Book of Jonah and parts of Deutero-Isaiah where Israel is called to be a light to the nations (42:6; 49:6). I personally would list Job among the "missionary literature" because in it a theophany produces repentance and restoration to a non-Israelite.

The Church and the Nations:
The Extent of Their Relationship

All of what has preceded this section would be of little significance if it was contradicted by the New Testament. What in fact we do find is the same pattern, embossed more deeply, colored more strongly, and of course in a much smaller frame. Bearing in mind that this is an outline, we will again emerge from the dissecting room and merely note the results.

Long concentration by the church on the central facts and teaching of the New Testament has understandably obscured the ubiquitous presence of the nations, their representatives, cultures, and faiths; but once the questions are raised, it is quickly revealed that the apostles and the early church were never an island. Like the Hebrew of the Old Testament, the language of the New Testament announces a foreign presence—Greek. But now it is a wholly non-Semitic presence. The authors of the New Testament writings learned their Old Testament in Greek; they lived in a Hellenized culture and finally thought through and explained their faith in the Greek language. The gospel did not have to wait until it emerged from Palestine before it began the encounter with the Greek "missionary" influence since the time of Alexander and even before. Greek religion, philosophy, literature, education, and sport are present in the New Testament writings as well as the immeasurable influence carried over by the language. But the Hellenic air was breathed in a Roman setting, and the Latin tongue and Latin poets were heard as well as Roman curses, Roman orders, and the rattling of Roman armor. As in the Old Testament a Pharaoh's oppression is at the heart of the Israelite creed, so a Roman procurator has found his way into the Apostles' Creed of the church. When Christians first confessed their faith they confessed it in Greek, and their faith was that Christ had risen from death on a Roman cross under the Roman

Pontius Pilate. A Roman census determined the place of his birth; wise men from the East visited the baby; he spoke with Samaritans, Greeks, Romans, and at least one Syro-Phoenician. After his death representatives of the nations came to Jerusalem, and some received the Holy Spirit. Before long the apostolic journeying to the ends of the earth begins, and the Book of Revelation returns to the themes of Genesis 10 and 11 as it envisages the nations—all tongues, tribes, and peoples—coming to the new Jerusalem. Even more than Israel in the Old Testament, the church lives its life in a cosmopolitan, international milieu.

The Church and the Nations: The Relationship Analyzed

The varied contacts between the new Israel and the nations are unquestionable. Does analysis show they form the same pattern as they did in the Old Testament?

The Church Existed and Exists for the Nations

The first Christians were Jews and were members of the old Israel and children of Abraham. Before long there were Christians who were like Abraham in that they were drawn out of the nations. From Greek and barbarian backgrounds they came to be part of that body of Christ which came to serve the world in the name of him who came to save it. Jesus had said that if he were lifted up he would draw all people unto him. The church was the instrument whereby he did the drawing; its members were called to be "fishers of men."

It is perhaps in Ephesians, where there is little explicit call to mission, that we see most clearly the church existing for, or on behalf of, mankind. Writing to the saints who are also faithful in Jesus Christ, Paul tells them they have been chosen to be holy and blameless before God, who has made known to them this purpose set forth in Christ "to unite all things in him, things in heaven and things on earth" (1:1–10). The Gentiles are now declared to be "fellow heirs, members of the same body, and partakers of the promise in Christ Jesus through the gospel." And Paul himself, the least of the saints, was called "to make all men see what is the plan of the mystery…; that through the church the manifold wisdom of God might now be made known to the principalities and powers in the heavenly places" (3:1–10). The church exists not only for the nations and their redemption but also for the forces that control them.

The Church's Life Was Lived Over Against the Nations

Jesus' life was a life of controversy ending with a confrontation first with the Jews and then with the Romans. Finally, he "suffered under Pontius Pilate, was crucified, died, and was buried." The same pattern is promised to the disciples: persecution is a source of blessing and absence of it a cause for concern. The history of the church in the New Testament, beginning with Acts, is a history of confrontation.

1. *The nations as enemies.* Beginning with the death of Christ, through apostolic suffering and martyrdom, to the persecution that lay behind Hebrews and Revelation, the nations were inimical to the church. To preach as Peter and Paul preached was to be beaten, stoned, and eventually killed; to be victorious was to endure the suffering and eventually die in the faith. To love one's enemies might result in their transformation, but meanwhile they remain enemies, and Christian love does not make them otherwise.

2. *The nations as a religious threat to the church.* Compromise with the surrounding faiths was the constant temptation of the early Christians. Meat offered to idols, the immorality accompanying idolatry, the pinch of incense to the Roman deity, these are but a few examples of the continuing threat to the new faith that came from the fervent and convenient religions with which the church was constantly in touch.

The Church as a Debtor to the Nations

Opposition and confrontation were not the whole story; the nations for whom the church existed provided much that the church needed, and the nature of the indebtedness was similar to that discovered in the Old Testament.

1. *Egypt protects the chosen.* The descendant of Jacob who was to be the true Israel descended, like Jacob, into Egypt and for the same purpose. Threatened by Herod, Mary and Joseph went into Egypt for protection, and thus the ambiguous relationship between Israel and Egypt was continued into the New Testament (and apparently is still with us. In 1980, Israel's Prime Minister Begin acted like Pharaoh, and Egypt's President Sadat provided a generous initiative that surely the Torah would commend).

2. *Cultural borrowing.* We have already spoken of the use of the Greek language and the concepts borrowed with it. To be more specific, John adopts the *logos* and adapts it to his own very special need. Words for "love," "righteousness," "covenant," and so forth, all trailing clouds of Greek meaning, are taken and modified with new content and usage. Greek philosophy is used by the writers of the Hebrews, and Greek literature is quoted by Paul.

3. *The nations as occasion for revelation.* A prophecy about the Messiah's birth is fulfilled through the instrumentality of the Augustan census. Roman law and Roman administration play an essential part in the crucifixion, as, later, Roman persecution provides us with the occasion of the eschatological vision known as Revelation. A significant link with the place of the nations in the Old Testament is found in John 12:20ff. Jesus has shown himself and been recognized by the Jews as king in accordance with the prophecy in Zechariah 9. But the same chapter, as well as other prophecies, requires recognition of the "Messiah" by the nations. The coming of the Greeks who want to see Jesus provides sufficient fulfillment of this prophecy for

Jesus to proceed with the explanation of his death, which appears to be directed toward his disciples and not toward the Greeks. The Greeks were the occasion of the revelation rather than its recipients.

4. *The nations as instruments of liberation.* Paul's appeal to his Roman citizenship is an example of this category. Nor unrelated is the sword of the authorities that is wielded on God's behalf to protect the good (Rom. 13:1ff.).

5. *The good pagans.* The good Samaritan, the centurion with a faith superior to Israel's, and the Ethiopian eunuch illustrate how this theme is continued in the New Testament.

The Church's Mission to the Nations

Matthew 28:19–20—the famous missionary text—makes explicit what is explicit elsewhere and implicit everywhere else in the New Testament. The Greek original, which means approximately "disciple the nations," is clearer than the usual translation. I am assuming that this point needs no elaboration, it is so obvious.

In Addition

If the New Testament, in large part, conforms to the four-fold design in the Old Testament, is this all that can be said, or is there something wholly new? Inasmuch as the New Testament is the fulfillment and the completion of the Old Testament—the head that the torso was lacking—there is nothing wholly new. At least in the light of Christ's coming and with hindsight, it can be seen that all had been indicated and pointed to (cf. Luke 24:25ff.). There is total continuity with the Old Testament and only with the Old Testament. Having said this, it must immediately be said that when the Word became flesh this was utterly new, and with it came the possibility of making all things new. But in what ways does this newness affect the relationships between God's work in creation and God's work in redemption, and within this the relationships between the elect and the nations?

Israel amidst the nations resembles the spies who first went into the promised land. They were of the same stuff as the Israelite army, integral to it, but they were not the invasion force. In Jesus the invasion has truly begun, the battle is on, and victory is assured if not yet secured.

After Christ, what is new is the certainty and clarity of being within a movement that has truly started and is not only expected. The "He who is to come" has come and is already at work, but the work is not different from that of Israel. The pattern remains, clearer but unchanged.

If the pattern is clearer, wherein lies the clarity? It is clearer that the chosen exist for the nations and for the world, and their mission is also clearer. The centripetal mission remains, but the most positive centrifugal mission now dominates, and the chief missionary is Jesus Christ. He is the sent one, the Apostle (Heb. 3:1), and the final mission to the nations is his (Matt. 25:31ff.; cf. Jeremias 1967). But if these two parts of the pattern are clear, so are the other two. There is equal clarity when the New Testament refers both to the religious threat from the nations and the necessity of confrontation. Apostasy results not only in death but also in eternal damnation, and, according to Hebrews, for those who have once spurned the gifts given by Christ there is no way of return. As to confrontation, it is the way of life a Christian must expect. The world will persecute of necessity, and killing a Christian will be regarded as a virtue. Persecution should not trouble the Christian; rather, the absence of it should be regarded as abnormal and a cause for concern. The apostles learned to live and rejoice to the accompaniment of conflict; they accepted that witness and martyrdom were synonymous.

The distinction without separation between God's "two activities" becomes more clear as the New Testament points to the mystery of the Trinity and the work of the Father and the work of the Son. Similarly, the hint we got in Hosea that dialogue begins in the Godhead is confirmed by the communion between the Son and the Father and most particularly in the Garden of Gethsemane and in the cry of dereliction from the cross.

Conclusions for Interfaith Dialogue
Critique

The above study—rectified and much improved—can serve as a set of guidelines to aid in assessing contemporary interfaith dialogue. As with the related problem of "indigenization," it is all too easy for dialogue to be under the control of prejudice, fashion, feeling of guilt, political influences, and so forth and to escape from a biblical anchorage. It is especially easy for "dialogue" to move toward the extreme of forgetting the finality of Christ or to its opposite of denying God's presence in the nations and the world he has created. At the present the former extreme is the greatest danger. How would the guidelines serve to preserve us from it?

God's presence in other faiths would be recognized as being of the order of creation and not of redemption, except insofar as redemption elements might be present "in reflection," because the two covenants in their interaction sometimes reflect each other.

Dialogue would be seen as an activity that in its complete form possesses recognition of all the four elements that are present in the biblical relationships. They would not all be present all the time, for they are not present all the time in the Bible, but they would be present in the understanding of dialogue held by the Christian participant in dialogue. In this, one would be frequently helped by one's partner, for some of the elements both positive and negative would be in the partner's mind and intentions as well. Interfaith dialogue without confrontation and without overt missionary activity might continue for a long time, how long being determined by the particular dialogue, but this would be partial dialogue and perhaps not particularly rewarding. True dialogue would be dialogue in which all four elements were actually or potentially present.

The Biblical Demand for Dialogue

I believe that this examination demonstrates that, in addition to the Bible's offering guidelines to prevent us from going too far astray in dialogue, it also voices an imperative to engage in dialogue, provided that it is biblically informed dialogue.

We have seen that in both the Testaments there is a kind of dialogue present within God. Hinted at in the Old Testament, it becomes more explicit in the New Testament. If this dialogue is viewed in the light of the early creeds, it can be described in part as dialogue between the "Father Almighty, maker of heaven and earth" and between the "Son, the Redeemer." In other words, it is a dialogue that is part of the interrelation of creation and new creation. The demand for dialogue, therefore, begins in the nature of God and is a concomitant of belief in the Trinity.

In both the Testaments God revealed himself as savior to his chosen people as they lived, moved, and had their being among the nations. The relationships between Israel/the church and God and between Israel/the church and the nations are two relationships that must not be treated as identical. Nevertheless, they are two relationships that are seldom seen apart. If, therefore, God has called his people out of the nations and continued to nourish them and instruct them as they interrelated and interwove with the nations, then is it not clear that such a process must continue and that what we call dialogue is part of it? Dialogue is not just permitted, nor is it merely a method of investigation and study, nor a prelude to conversion—although it can be these. It is a part of God's will for the church. It is partially through dialogue that God's call, nourishment, and instruction are still mediated to the church so that the church may better be that in which the nations find blessing.

But we can and must go further, and to do this a more biblical method than analysis is preferred. I have chosen a passage from the Old Testament, and with it as guide I want to maintain that true dialogue belongs to the church's identity and essence as well as to its nourishment and instruction.

Genesis 32:22 tells of Jacob's discovering his identity as Israel. He does this by wrestling with an unknown assailant who blesses him, lames him, and gives him his identity. Only at the end is the assailant recognized as possessing the face of God. Rabbi Marmur, relying on an interpretation of Rashi, sees Jacob wrestling with the guardian angel of Esau, Esau symbolizing the Gentiles. Applying this to the questions of Jewish identity, Marmur says that Israel is only Israel when she is locked in wrestling with the Gentiles. When she refuses to wrestle, either by retreating into the ghetto or by being absorbed into the Gentiles, Israel reverts to being Jacob. Israel's identity depends upon being constantly face to face in wrestle with the Gentiles. Apply this to the church, the new Israel. The church is the church only when it is wrestling with the nations. "Pietistic" retreat and "liberal" accommodation to the nations are equally ways of ceasing to be the church. But who are the nations? They are the brother, in ways superior to the church, as Esau was superior to Jacob. The church's object is to "strive and prevail," but the prevailing is more in behalf of the nations than in its own behalf, for it is the church that is lamed, and the nations will eventually receive blessing only if the church is truly the church. And of course it is in the wrestling that the church is blessed, and in the wrestling that it sees the face of God in the enemy who is the church's "twin."

Some will reject this type of presentation, and in this particular instance they may be right. However, to reject the method *in toto* is to reject a biblical mode of communication. But, assuming that in the story there is encapsulated a truth that belongs to the whole history of both Israel and the church, and assuming that my interpretation has not wholly distorted that truth, then let the story be a parable that points to the church's dialectical duty.

The church approaches other faiths acknowledging and rejoicing in all the true virtue, goodness, faith, and devotion to be found in them because God the creator is present in them. It also approaches peoples of other faiths as brothers and sisters in whom lies our own blessing, our own calling and identity, and in whom we see the face of God. At the same time, we seek ultimately to prevail, although we know that we will suffer in the wrestling dialogue. But we must prevail for God's sake and for the sake of the nations.

5

A Missionary Hermeneutic of Scripture

Some of the Questions

In previous chapters I have linked the church, Trinity, and scripture in mission and unity. I have assumed a missionary understanding of the Trinity in the concept of the *missio dei* and a missionary understanding of the church. I have argued for a missionary understanding of scripture. Dare we argue for a missionary hermeneutic of the canon? What follows are merely the notes for an introduction to the prolegomenon of any future missionary hermeneutic. That is all I claim for it. I leave the introduction and the prolegomenon to other people.

Against the background of the broad sweep of canon and mission issues, I want to concentrate on one part and begin to examine the possibility of what might be called a missionary hermeneutic. If there is a close connection between the canon and mission, as has been suggested, and if valid mission is dependent on its having a full canonical basis, and if it is threatened by anything less than the whole counsel of God as revealed in the canon, then is it reasonable to ask whether there is a corresponding dependence in the other direction? In other words, if mission requires a canonical basis, does the canon in some ways demand a missionary hermeneutic if it is more fully to release its riches so that treasures both old and new might emerge?

Earlier in this century the church discovered or rediscovered that mission and the unity of the church were inseparable and interdependent. Somewhat later the Roman Catholic Church in Vatican II through *Lumen Gentium* suggested that mission has the key that opened a little wider the door to the mysterious nature of the church. Is it now appropriate to ask whether mission and the unity and nature of scripture are not similarly related, and so related that mission is the key and clue that will help us appreciate in new ways the totality of scripture?

The church has known Platonic and Aristotelian hermeneutics; allegorical, existential, anthropological, and evolutionary hermeneutics. This century has seen national-socialist, Marxist, and apartheid hermeneutics. There are pietistic and moralistic hermeneutics. The dominant form of interpretation for almost two centuries has been controlled by the historical-critical ascendancy with its various progeny of atomism, geneticism, primitivism, literary analysis, and so forth, and the canonization of the diachronic method. To speak of a missionary hermeneutic is not to deny value indiscriminately to all of this, and many other hermeneutical starting points. It is first of all to say: "Here is an approach to scripture that has been insufficiently considered, and in most areas, beginning with the study and the classroom, almost wholly neglected. Let us at least put it alongside the others and ask whether it does not deserve a place on a very long list." Having said that, it may then be possible to advance a little further and even to ask whether the missionary approach might not be put near the top of the list so that it acts normatively in relation to some, perhaps all the others.

Such a proposal will not be welcomed in many of the realms of biblical scholarship, but some support for it certainly may be found there and even perhaps among the increasing numbers outside the discipline who are now contributing to the literature on scripture. I see support coming particularly from biblical scholars who write on canonical criticism, theologians who stress narrative theology, and literary critics who nowadays are more concerned with the synchronic than with the diachronic understanding. As this chapter is a mere hors d'oeuvre, I will concentrate on one main argument, and that a mere morsel, with no suggestion that the case rests on these alone.

Approaching the Argument

Some writers on the canon, accepting that the intentional fallacy has indeed been a fallacy, concentrate on interpreting the canon in its present form without too much emphasis on how the canon came into being. They are led by Brevard Childs. Others, and chief among them is J. A. Sanders, pay most attention to the process of canonization. They ask questions about the nature and function of canon. Why was a canon necessary? What was its *Sitz im Leben* within the believing communities that brought a canon into being and eventually made it central in both Judaism and the church? They are also, of course, concerned with the historical rise and historical development of the canon, concentrating not so much on the introductory questions of source as the more theological questions of nature and function. Also, they bypass exegesis of the finished text— immanent to the other parts of the new canonical movement led so remarkably by Brevard Childs. This concentration on the process they designate as canonical criticism.

Canonical criticism is in part a corrective to the Enlightenment influences that to a large extent de-canonized the Bible. The true marriage between ecclesia and academia had been dissolved in the eighteenth century. The Bible had been effectively removed from the pulpit and lectern and locked in the study. With the dominance of the historical-critical approach and the rise of primitivism, the

Bible was not only locked in the study; it was locked into the past. The church was, to all intents and purposes, without a scripture, and the believing communities had been living with less and less belief in consequence. They had lost a scripture and in return received a library of *biblia*, read as a neuter plural, each one of which was then further divided into fragmentary pericopes, some of which were the original deposit and of greater value than the later, somewhat spurious, additions. What little remained of the concept of authoritative canon was attached loosely to certain events, persons, and collections of *ipsissima verba*, most of which were extremely conjectural.

In reading the Bible, the church was directed to anything but the text itself. Bible reading became scriptural avoidance as readers were directed to events, themes, principles, concepts, and so forth. Canonical criticism is an attempt to take the place of the beadle (I speak here as a Presbyterian), who brings the Bible into the church, into the midst of the believing community, and places it on the lectern or the pulpit, from which it has been temporarily absent. Part of this canonical-critical beadle's task is seen to be a careful examination of the place of canon in Judaism and the church. Why was there or is there a canon, and why was there or is there a particular canon? I propose to draw heavily on the research so far done in canonical criticism to ask questions concerning canon and mission. In the questions that Sanders and others are asking, in the answers they receive, and in the hypotheses they advance, what, if anything, is there that can be related to the mission of the church? Is it possible that among the *raison d'être* of the canon concepts and of the specific canons we can find cause to say that they were called into being for a missionary purpose? In the small fraction of the literature I have examined so far, I have rarely, if ever, encountered the word "mission." The canon renewers are not, on the surface at least, missionary minded; but the absence of a word is not necessarily equivalent to the absence of all it connotes. Is it possible that behind the foliage of uncommon words there lurks the sly shade of missionary intention? If mission needs a canonical basis, does the canon correspondingly depend upon mission and a missionary understanding? Is the purpose and object of the canon mission? Without mission does it lose much of its significance? Historically, the growth of the Old Testament is related to the two destructions of Jerusalem, 587 B.C. and 70 A.D. But such facts answer few questions about the reasons for, and causes of the canon, and the appearances of canon and the need for canon. Perhaps as H. Von Campenhausen suggests, there are liturgical factors. Josephus may have been correct in stressing popular demand. Morton Smith (1987) opts for a simple political solution—the Yahweh-only party won the day. Or was it the overwhelming authority of a name that ensured canonicity: Moses, Solomon, David, or John, Peter, or Paul? Or do we have Esther because Purim was so firmly established in a community that they had to have a reason for it? Canonical criticism pursues its questions at a deeper level and produces a variety of results.

Beginning the Argument

Humanly speaking, the canon concept appears because of the needs of the believing community, and the particular canon appears because of the continuing needs and experiences of that community. Under God, the believing community creates the canon, and then, in turn, the canon maintains, supports, and continues the community. There is first the human wrestle, the passionate dialogue and questioning, the Jacob-like seeking for blessing and survival in the midst of fear. Only later is it possible to say, "The Lord is in this place," or to recognize that you have seen the face of God. There is a very human element susceptible to historical and theological probing.

In Ezekiel 33 the exiles ask, "How shall we live?" The prophetic answer is, in effect, that Israel is Israel by the judgments of God; but there soon follows the redemption and miraculous resurrection of Israel in chapter 37. The canon is being created within the believing community by a massive process of dialogue that is ultimately seen to be dominated by the word of God and the deeds of God. The canon testifies to the one true God, but it is a parliamentary testimony. The parliamentary debate is all there in the Bible, both government and opposition, and it is rarely a loyal opposition. The canonical witness is not monophone. The opposition often seems to defeat the sovereign ruler, and sometimes it is not immediately obvious on which side is truth and which side falsity. In fact, you can tell only within the totality of a canon when the canon is complete. Scripture is not monophonic or monovalent. It is ultimately monotheising, but it is not wholly monotheistic. The monotheism is surrounded by and wrapped up in polytheism and idolatry as though somehow they have a place in the testimony. The canon is a strange example of pluralism that, only in its completeness, bears witness to the one true God. Fragmented, its alienated parts, robbed of the self-rectifying, self-modifying, self-correcting totality, can become paradigms for heresy and falsehood. Alone, Balaam's ass can only bray the wrong questions. Job, on its own, is an argument against saving history and for natural theology. A God who only hardened Pharaoh's heart would be a monster; Isaiah 6:9ff., an incomprehensible disaster, Ecclesiastes a mortuary aroma and little else, Jonah a music hall turn.

Then what, positively, does the dialogue, the Bible's inner friction, say about the nature and function of canon? I will look at only some of the conclusions relevant mainly to the Old Testament. Much more could be said about the New Testament. This is, after all, merely an hors d'oeuvre.

The canonical Torah is a product of the Exile, as, according to Jeremias, was also the beginning of the Jewish mission that eventually flourished so greatly in the time of Christ. So the canon and the Jewish mission are a *post hoc.* Are they, perhaps, a *propter hoc* suggesting a link between canon and mission from the earliest days? Israel had lost virtually everything in 587 B.C. and questioned everything. As we have seen in Ezekiel 33, there was the very question of life itself. Was the living God, the source of life, still with them? Or was God also a victim defeated by the gods of Babylon? Israel's life and the life of God were inseparable. But if God was alive and they were alive, and not dead bones, how did they relate, and who were they without land and without temple and without sacrifice and priestly ministration? There was also the question of identity. Were they still Israel, and, if they were, what kind of Israel were they in an unclean land? What was their way of life and their way of worship? How did they relate to God, to each other, to the enemy, to nature, and to uncleanness, and, perhaps above all, how did they relate to the future? Was there continuity with the past, and was there hope for the coming generations? All the great questions were present: life, identity, lifestyle, survival, and continuity. Overarching them all was the question of what to believe about God.

Israel had come into being through covenant that rested on a story. She was the creature of that story, living by it and living out of it; but the old, old story of Yahweh and his love seemed to have lost its power. Was the story still true and was it still applicable, or should it be hung with the harps on the willows?

More on the Canon

Sanders sees such questions always lying behind the need for a canon: life, identity, lifestyle, continuity, and hope. The questions are addressed to the truth and authenticity of the story that has lain behind their life, identity, lifestyle, continuity, and hope in previous generations. To such questions the canonical process responds with two major aspects—stability and flexibility. The stability element ensures continuity with the past. There must be faithfulness to the primal story, and this faithfulness provides stability and security in the present and promises it in the future. The stability rests on the enduring stability of the God who is the source of all, and on the truth of the story that underlies and conveys this relationship. The stability of the canonical text is a somewhat later development. What is of first importance is the stability and continuity of the community. But the stability is paired with extreme adaptability that at times can even be ambiguous about whether the story is the Exodus story or the David story. The adaptability, the flexibility, is essential to meet the challenges of new situations and changing circumstances. The adaptability at times is so great, so elastic, that on the surface it threatens the stability element, as when in Isaiah 43 the prophet says, "Remember not the former things.... Behold, I am doing a new thing" (vv. 18–19). Only the context redeems this from heresy.

The greatest exercise of the force of adaptability is, of course, evident in the way the Hebrew scriptures are appropriated by the writers of the New Testament and the early church. The Hebrew scriptures were the scriptures of Jesus Christ and the only scriptures of the early church. They were authoritative, and appeal was made to them at every turn for validation of the religious upheaval that was taking place. Everything was grounded in their truth. The "historical" truth of what was happening depended on the historical truth of Israel's Bible. But this paradoxically results in the virtual destruction of the historical significance of the Hebrew scriptures as they are turned into an unintended prologue to the New Testament. Having become part of the Christian Bible, the historical context of the Hebrew scriptures, with a few exceptions, is largely ignored. Beginning with our Lord himself, they are now seen as a prophecy and preparation for the coming of

Jesus. Old Israel's function, it is now assumed, was to prepare for the true Israel, Jesus, and the new Israel, the
church. The old Exodus, with its old interpretation,
becomes a threat because the new liberation, the new
Exodus, has come in Christ.

The Jews, who do not recognize what is happening and
do not greet the Messiah, can no longer understand their
scriptures. A veil now covers their faces. The Hebrew scriptures that are instrumental in creating the New Testament
are made to die to the church as they are turned into the
Old Testament. In Christ the canon of Judaism no longer
exists. Its very ordering is restructured as the prophets are
taken out of the center of the Hebrew scriptures and put
next to the gospels. This, in a sense, is symbolic of what
was happening to the Hebrew scriptures. Historically, the
Old Testament is prior to the New Testament. Logically and
theologically, the New Testament is prior because it is in
the light of the new covenant that the old is seen to be old.
To refer again to the illustration in Revelation, the twelve
gates in the new Jerusalem are named after the twelve
tribes, and the apostles are the foundation. This symbolizes
the theological priority of the New Testament. Once they
are recognized as two parts of the greater whole, the canon
of the church, the two Testaments are mutually creating
and interdependent. When this happened, the Hebrew
scriptures lost their former significance, as shown so
poignantly by our Lord's saying that the Jews searched the
scriptures for life. They were asking the old canon the right
questions but were not getting the right answers because
the adaptability of the canon-creating process had overtaken
them. Their scriptures still held the key to life—and identity, lifestyle, continuity, and hope—but only if they were
now seen to be the Old Testament, which took its place
alongside the New Testament in the new, greater whole, the
church's canon.

We will look back briefly at the Bible as a whole in a moment. Meanwhile, let us pause to ask whether this thumbnail sketch of a fraction of the canonical process has anything to say that is relevant to our main question of canon and mission. Are they so closely related that it is difficult to think of them apart? Is it possible in any sense to say that the canon exists for mission and that the *missio dei*, the *missio christi*, and the *missio ecclesiae* are in great part the explanation for the existence of the canon? Dare we advance a step further as we query whether Christian mission can effectively exist without the canon and also whether we can effectively understand the canon unless we are constantly aware of the missionary imperative. Is mission hidden beneath the nonmissionary language of the canonizing process?

The Heart of the Matter

Although recognizing the danger of seeing Helen in every woman, is it wholly wrong to see in the canonizing process some, if not all, of the essentials of mission? The human quest is a series of questions: who am I and how do I live, where am I, and why am I? How do my present and past relate, and what is my future? With whom do I journey, and how do I journey? Such questions are part of the human side of mission. Christianity affirms that the Christian canon contains the divine response to these questions. Part of that response is to judge the questions and to reform them in the light of the answer in Christ, which is not only the right answer but the source of all right questioning.

The canon and its contents come to us as the answer to all our seeking. It witnesses to the whole truth of God. It carries the whole story that is necessary for all humankind at all times. It carries the variety that is necessary to meet all eventualities in all ages. Therefore, it

comes in paradox and tension, in ambiguity and ambiva-
lence, in contrast and contradiction. It comes not merely
to convey past facts, although it does that; not merely to
convey an original intent or original intention, although it
does that. It provides an ethos, an identity, an understanding in a meaningless world, an order in a disorderly world.
Somehow the ambiguity of the canon provides the certainty that all people need and the believing community in any
age can possess. In its ambiguity it is our bulwark in an
ambiguous world. Its apparent unreality and irrelevance to
the so-called real world witnesses to the true reality that
judges and redeems. It bears the story that gives life and
provides survival and continuity. It carries the power and
authority that challenge the destructive forces about us. It
judges the novel and the changing and enables us to reject
or redeem what existence presents to us. It does this by a
proclamation that is both complex and simple, stable and
adaptable, certain and flexible, and that has Christ at its
center. Is this mission, and, if so, is mission of the essence
of the Christian canon?

What I have said is the smallest beginning of the pursuit.
Much more could be said arising out of the canonization of
the Old Testament and even more if the question is carried
through to the emergence of the New Testament canon.
Similarly, the interdependent relationship between canon
and mission and the canon's need for a missionary understanding would appear more clearly from the rise of the
total Christian canon, which includes the transformation
of the Old Testament. It includes a study of the rise of the
total Christian canon, which includes the transformation
of the Old Testament or transformation of the Hebrew
scriptures into the Old Testament.

The Question Backward

Almost all I have said so far has been in connection with
the canonical process. A second way of asking the question

is to move beyond the creating process and come to the finished product. Is there support from the shape, ordering, and nature of the finished canon for this interdependence of mission and canon and for the need for a missionary hermeneutic? As said earlier, this quest may follow at least two approaches.

The first turns to the continuing themes and ordering of the contents of the canon. Examples of these, which are more obvious to the literary critics than to biblical scholars, include:

1. The canon moves from creation to new creation, from the heavens and the earth to the new heavens and the new earth, from a rural Eden to an urban Eden. This movement of renewal, restoration, and redemption is through a sent nation, a sent son, and a sent community.

2. The ubiquitous descent and ascent pattern that belongs to the whole Bible, the pattern that Northrop Frye has taught us to call the U pattern, belongs to the whole Bible and to almost every part; almost every part gives support to the descent and ascent pattern of the incarnation found supremely in Philippians 2:5–11 and finds its deepest explanation in the death and resurrection of Christ. The pattern permeating the whole is the pattern of the sent Son witness to the sent nation and the sent church.

3. The canon is about distorted relationships—God and creation, God and man/woman, person and person, humankind and creation, the person and the self—and their restoration in Christ. Christ is the reconciler, witnessed to by the reconciled and reconciling community.

4. The four promises to Abraham culminating in the blessings to the nations and often seen as the beginning of mission have also been seen by David J. A. Clines as providing the architectonic structure of the canon.

5. The canon is ordered so that all before Christ focuses on him and all after him radiates from him. But how will

they hear without a preacher? There has to be narrative and witness, therefore mission.

The second approach is to consider the nature of the contents. Some examples are these:

1. The whole is narrative about those sent and requires narration by those who are also sent. The requirement is made known by those two complementary spheres of the whole, law and promise. We are commanded to proclaim and witness. At the same time, it is not only a command; it is a promise. You shall be my witnesses.

2. The whole canon centers around the words and deeds of the personal God that have to be communicated by persons. The canon is inseparable from certain events that can be made known only by personal narration, personal acceptance, and personal commitment.

3. The clear message of the canon is a monotheizing message, but it appears in a sea of polytheism and idolatry, both within and without the chosen people. As noted above, the whole debate is present; all the dialogues are represented. The one God is witnessed to as creator and redeemer in the midst of all that makes belief in God unlikely and would destroy his believers. It is unwelcome testimony in a resisting environment. "He came to his own and his own received him not," but the darkness, not comprehending him, did not overwhelm him. The light shone. This means that the very presentation of Father, Son, and Holy Spirit is a missionary presentation. Trinitarian monotheism in the canon comes to us as a missionary resistance movement. It is a counterculture within the Bible itself. The canon is given to the church in a fallen world in an apostolic missionary form but with the assurance that the light shines in the darkness with a brightness independent of our comprehension.

There is yet at least one more way of beginning the investigation. So far we have started with the canon, its coming into being and its final shape. Then we asked whether some of its contents are missionary and whether mission is the essence of the canon. This approach would have to be balanced and modified by beginning in mission. A weakness in what I have said is that there has been no definition of mission. In a proper study this would have to be rectified. Would a Roman Catholic understanding of mission, with its strong ecclesiological emphasis, point us toward the canons. Or would a charismatic, or an orthodox? Have I been operating with a Reformed view or merely a Beeby prejudice? What does missionary hermeneutic mean and involve?

First, it is not an exclusive hermeneutic. That would be an unwarranted reductionism. A canon that has come through every kind of dialogue—dialogue within God, God and Israel, God and the nations, Israel and the nations, God in creation, God in redemption, God and creation, humankind and creation, the person and the self—allows for a variety of starting points. The question is not one of exclusion but of priority.

Second, a missionary hermeneutic should have high priority. A missionary hermeneutic presupposes a canonical hermeneutic that gives full range to the inner dialectics and recognizes that the missionary demands were not the sole demands in the process of canon formation. The canon is also a response to ethical, liturgical, social, and political demands, but these are partial and secondary in relation to the all-embracing needs and demands of the church's mission.

Third, a high priority—perhaps the highest priority—for the missionary hermeneutic is assumed, for it may be so claimed because a missionary canonical hermeneutic is one that takes place within a holistic narrative that is supremely missionary.

Mission Is More Than Concept

Fourth, a missionary hermeneutic means that the missionary motivation should have a normative function. It might function negatively, discouraging hermeneutical

factors that are less significant and certainly not dominant. Some hermeneutics are controlled by philosophical
or ideological concepts. They may be too conceptual,
reflective, even speculative. Although not denying them a
place, priority should be given to a missionary hermeneutic because it combines the conceptual with action. It
demands a hermeneutic that does not end in thought but
moves to decision and action. It is not governed by the
world's need but meets that need as it is seen and interpreted in the light of the gospel. It is not satisfied with anything less than the most significant, demanding, sacrificial,
all-embracing praxis but it does not begin in praxis, or with
any praxis-dominated ideology. Positively, it can claim to
find its center within scripture and not outside it. At this
center it is saying in the Old Testament, "Holy, holy, holy
is the Lord of hosts." It is saying in the New Testament in
Revelation 4 that the angelic host does the same, day and
night, without ceasing. But throughout, it says this to
unclean prophets and apostles in the midst of unclean people. It says it in the face of all the idols, demons, principalities, and powers, all the pseudo-sacreds and god-substi-
tutes. It calls us to make the same affirmation and promises that we shall do so. If this is done, then all the earth will
be full of God's glory.

If I were a postmodernist or a literary critic, I would be
able to say the gist of much of what I have said above in a
scholarly setting and be accepted. A postmodernist presentation would present it as one story among a myriad, all
equally true, all equally untrue. The literary critic would be
seen merely as speaking about the meaning of a text, and
hearers would know that the critic was not concerned with
a truth claim. To present it as a convinced Christian who
believes that it is ontologically true and is about the one
true big story—metanarrative if you like—would not be
academic. Perhaps you do not accept it, academically, but
to believe it and to confine it to the church alone bring two

results. It closes the door to real mission and to mission to the culture; and, second, in Europe it is resulting in the closing of the church door. But if the canon is about the Almighty, the King of creation, and if its main thrust is a missionary thrust, then we have to storm the ramparts of all those places that preserve and protect the current cultural paradigms so that we may convey it from generation to generation. We have to do this in order to claim the root paradigms of our society in the name of Christ. If Jesus Christ is Lord at all, he is Lord of all. Amen!

References Cited

Ariarajah, Wesley. 1985. *The Bible and People of Other Faiths*. Geneva: WCC Publications.

Bosch, David J. 1991. *Transforming Mission*. Maryknoll: Orbis Books.

Caird, George B. 1963. *Saint Luke*. London: Pelican Press.

Childs, Brevard. 1974. *A Commentary on Exodus*. London: SCM Press.

Clines, David. J. A. 1978. *The Theme of the Pentateuch*. Sheffield: University of Sheffield.

Cullmann, Oscar. 1967. *Salvation in History*. London: SCM Press.

Hulme, T. E. 1924. *Speculations*. London: Kegan Paul.

Jeremias, Joachim. 1967. *Jesus' Promise to the Nations*. London: SCM Press.

Kaufmann, Y. 1961. *The Religion of Israel*. London: Georgle, Allen & Unwin.

Leech, Kenneth. 1986. *Spirituality and Pastoral Care*. London: Sheldon Press.

Levenson, Jon D. 1993. *The Hebrew Bible: The Old Testament and Historical Criticism*. Louisville: Westminster/John Knox Press.

Lindbeck, George A. 1989. The Church's Mission to Postmodern Culture. In *Postmodern Theology: Christian Faith in a Pluralist World*, edited by Frederic B. Burnham, 37-55. San Francisco: Harper & Row.

Linnemann, Eta. 1990. *Historical Criticism of the Bible.* Grand Rapids: Baker Book House.

Morgan, Robert, and John Barton. 1988. *Biblical Interpretation.* New York: Oxford University Press.

Polanyi, Michael 1958. *Personal Knowledge.* London: Routledge & Kegan Paul.

Reumann, John Henry Paul. 1973. *Creation and New Creation: The Past, Present and the Future of God's Creative Activity.* Minneapolis: Augsburg Press.

Sanders, J. A. 1972. *Torah and Canon.* Philadelphia: Fortress Press.

———. 1987. *From Sacred Story to Sacred Text.* Philadelphia: Fortress Press.

Smith, Morton. 1987. *Palestinian Parties and Politics that Shaped the Old Testament.* London: SCM Press.

Smith, Wilfred Cantwell. 1993. *What Is Scripture?* Minneapolis: Fortress Press.

Steiner, George. 1989. *Real Presences.* London: Faber & Faber.

Von Rad, Gerhard. 1957 German trans. 1962. *Old Testament Theology, Vol. I.* London: Oliver and Boyd.

———. 1960 German trans. 1965. *Old Testament Theology, Vol. II.* Harper & Row.

———. 1958 German trans. 1966 *The Problem of the Hexateuch and Other Essays.* London: Oliver and Boyd.

———. 1956 German trans. 1961. *Genesis.* London: SCM Press.

Wink, Walter. 1973. *The Bible in Human Transformation.* Philadelphia: Fortress Press.